Praise for *Shadow Magick Spellbook*

"*Shadow Magick Spellbook* is exceptionally relevant to the times we live in. It contains inclusive workings for every human navigating the modern world through the lens of Witchcraft, providing guided steps for traversing the complicated layers of the shadow. Raven provides practical instructions, sprinkled with unique insights that can only come with personal experience and a functional knowledge of shadow work. With the added perspective of guest writers, this is the ultimate comprehensive guide to shadow magick."

—**KATE FREULER,** author of *Of Blood and Bones* and *Magic at the Crossroads*

"This is one of the most in-depth and advanced spellbooks we've read in many years. It's practical, insightful, and clearly comes from the author's own experiences. It's not just a spellbook, it's a guide to self-healing and discovery through holistic practice. Whether you're an existing magical practitioner wanting to go that stage further, or you're looking for a book that will help you with healing yourself or others, we can't recommend this one enough. It's a life changer!"

—**JANET FARRAR AND GAVIN BONE,** authors of *Progressive Witchcraft* and *Lifting the Veil*

"A lively and well-written cornucopia of simple spells for everyday purposes."

—**PETER J. CARROLL,** author of *Liber Null & Psychonaut*

"Whether you're facing trauma, exploring the unknown, or trying to reconnect with parts of yourself that feel lost, these practical workings can light your way through the darkness and help you find renewed strength and clarity. This guide is a nurturing resource for witches, empaths, and all those on a journey of self-discovery, supporting you in deep healing, protection, and personal growth."
—**JOHN J. COUGHLIN,** author of *Out of the Shadows*

"Raven Digitalis provides you with magical tools to support your personal journey of growth. It includes well-written spells along with helpful information to improve the efficacy of your magick. I highly recommend this book for both experienced and novice magic practitioners."
—**FRATER TENEBRIS,** author of *The Philosophy of Dark Paganism*

"Raven Digitalis brings the psychological technique of shadow work back to its spiritual origins. His is a magickal approach designed to complement treatment from healthcare professionals. As readers integrate repressed parts of themselves in a quest for wholeness, Raven's caring for them is very evident, guiding them every step of the way."
—**TONY MIERZWICKI,** author of *Hellenismos*

"*Shadow Magick Spellbook* expertly presents shadow work with rare intelligence and genuine compassion. Raven offers both theoretical insight and a wealth of practical techniques for healing personal and collective wounds, including self-forgiveness, trauma, grief, anger, addiction, social anxiety, social media, and the shadow of nature, to name just a few. This book is sure to shed light on previously unknown aspects of the reader's shadow and provide numerous practices for integrating them."

—**JOE MONTELEONE,** founder of Tarot Mysticism Academy and author of *Tarot Mysticism*

"Raven's book is simply the best grimoire I have ever seen on shadow work, emphasizing ethical responsibility rarely seen in magickal tomes. I will be recommending it for all our students."

—**OBERON ZELL,** founder of the Grey School of Wizardry

SHADOW MAGICK SPELLBOOK

SHADOW MAGICK SPELLBOOK

Spells, Charms & Rituals for Positive Change

RAVEN DIGITALIS

WOODBURY, MINNESOTA

© Photo by Angela Clausen

About the Author

Raven Digitalis (USA) is an award-winning author best known for his "empath's trilogy," consisting of *The Empath's Oracle, Esoteric Empathy*, and *The Everyday Empath*, as well as the "shadow trilogy" of *A Gothic Witch's Oracle, A Witch's Shadow Magick Compendium*, and *Goth Craft*. Originally trained in Georgian Witchcraft, Raven has been an earth-based practitioner since 1999, a priest since 2003, a Freemason since 2012, and an empath all of his life. He holds a degree in cultural anthropology from the University of Montana, jointly operated a nonprofit Pagan temple for sixteen years, and is also a professional tarot reader, editor, Reiki practitioner, and animal rights advocate.

www.ravendigitalis.com
social media: @ravendigitalis

First Edition
First Printing, 2026

Book design by Rordan Brasington
Cover design by Kevin R. Brown
Editing by Sophia Kurtz
Interior Ilustrations by Llewellyn Art Department: 29, 35, 54, 57, 62, 69, 101, 102, 117, 122, 132, 142, 145, 158, 172, 174, 197, 205, 217

Library of Congress Cataloging-in-Publication Data (Pending)
ISBN: 978-0-7387-8137-2

Llewellyn Publications
A Division of Llewellyn Worldwide Ltd.
2143 Wooddale Drive
Woodbury, MN 55125-2989
www.llewellyn.com

Printed in the United States of America

GPSR Representation:
UPI-2M PLUS d.o.o., Medulićeva 20, 10000 Zagreb, Croatia
matt.parsons@upi2mbooks.hr

Other Books by this author

A Gothic Witch's Oracle (Crossed Crow Books, 2025)

The Empath's Oracle (Llewellyn Publications, 2022)

The Everyday Empath (Llewellyn Publications, 2019)

Esoteric Empathy (Llewellyn Publications, 2016)

A Witch's Shadow Magick Compendium (Crossed Crow Books, 2022)

Planetary Spells & Rituals (Llewellyn Publications, 2010)

Goth Craft (Llewellyn Publications, 2007)

Magick for Empaths (Pagan Portals series) (Moon Books, 2025)

Black Magick (fiction anthology) (Moon Books, 2025)

Disclaimer

Welcome to *Shadow Magick Spellbook.* I hope your time with this book proves worthwhile for you now and throughout life's path. But first, it's time to listen up!

There are particular warnings, concerns, and points of consideration that every reader should be aware of before approaching this book's material. This might seem lengthy and possibly overcautious, but it's necessary to state the following straight away.

This book's advice and its contents are not substitutes for professional medical or therapeutic advice. Neither myself, the publisher, any bookseller, nor anyone associated with this book's publication or distribution may be held liable for undesirable effects that arise as a result of using the information in this book.

This book and its contents are not intended to diagnose, treat, cure, or prevent any disease, disorder, condition, or ailment. This book is not a substitution for professional healthcare or medically prescribed allopathic or naturopathic medicine.

Professional treatment is quite often a significant component of successful shadow work. We must become our own advocates with the same care we'd extend to others. As with most shadow work, professional therapy, counseling, and coaching can be a tremendous ally. Trained professionals can be of great assistance, and the quality ones *want* to help others because it's their life's calling and passion.

Please seek licensed professional medical and/or therapeutic treatment for mental or physical health conditions, addiction or substance dependency issues, or ongoing conditions such as depression, anxiety, and anger.

I speak from experience when I say that therapy and medicinal intervention can change one's life for the better. Some of these spells and rituals deal with trauma, depression, anxiety, anger, and psychological distress. There comes a point when professional treatment is not only advisable but is necessary. For example, if you suffer social anxiety and have discovered that it hinders everyday functioning, know that you're not alone—please seek assistance from a psychiatric physician and/or licensed therapist.

If you are dealing with someone whose mental health conditions or behaviors are threatening to your physical or emotional wellbeing, please seek proper treatment to help you separate from the dangerous individual or situation. If you are in danger or are experiencing any level of abuse, do not hesitate to seek immediate assistance from law enforcement, shelters, and local departments of health and human service.

Several of these spells use bodily fluids, including blood. If you have a history of self-harm, it is advisable to shy away from using your own blood in ritual. Intentionally focusing your own energetic life-force is a perfectly viable substitute for blood magick. If anything in this book could be potentially triggering, injurious, or illegal, just don't do it.

Herbal suggestions in this book, whether meant for consumption or external use, are not substitutes for prescription medications or professional medical assistance. Be aware of any and all contraindications if you choose to ingest herbs as a tea, tincture, or topical ointment. Check in with an herbalist, naturopath, or doctor if you are planning on consuming an herbal preparation regularly, especially if recent changes in health have occurred. This includes medication changes, surgeries, pregnancy, and lactation.

Research your current medications and supplements to see if harmful interactions may occur as a result of consuming certain teas, tinctures, or herbal remedies. Never consume poisonous herbs, don't touch them with bare hands, and avoid skin contact.

When ritualizing in the natural world, be sure not to disrupt any ecosystems. Only forage or wild harvest what is sustainable. Don't bury or leave behind anything that is not biodegradable, and try to pick up litter wherever and whenever you see it. If working in a cemetery, do not disrupt any gravesites or jump fences. Exercise caution and respect. Use your best judgment in any situation.

Take precautions when using ritual tools suggested in this book. Don't allow candles or incense to burn unattended, be mindful of poisonous or irritating substances, don't break any laws, don't piss off the neighbors, don't harm your body, don't trespass, and so on. When in doubt about any spell's procedure, either don't do it or modify accordingly.

Neither myself, nor the publishers, nor the gods can be held liable for readers not taking necessary precautions, making risky choices, or triggering psychological issues. Be aware, be respectful, and use your head. You've got this!

P.S. For readers who have suffered with lifelong depression, anxiety, OCD, or debilitating psychological distress, I recommend speaking with a medical professional about Transcranial Magnetic Stimulation (TMS). I and others I know have had remarkable success with this "brain magnet" treatment, which was developed relatively recently and is the go-to procedure for these conditions in numerous European countries. In the US, Medicaid will indeed cover this series of 36 awkward-yet-rewarding treatments if you can produce proper documentation of tried and failed medicinal and therapeutic history. If you or someone you know suffers from these conditions, I encourage you to research the process and incredible success rate of TMS treatment.

Acknowledgments

Deepest gratitude to my amazing friends and family for the love, support, and inspiration—particularly to my mamallama, Barbara Holmes-Smith, for being this book's honorary "spellchecker!" Endless appreciation as well to my dad, Jeff, for the heartfelt cheer throughout my writing career—there's no need to understand all the weird things I write about; your support means the world to me!

Dear nephew Liam, sorry I couldn't incorporate your awesome anonymous messages into this book or my online articles; publishers have their own rules of operation. Love to you, to my fabulous niece Elsie, and of course to my brilliant brother and sister Justin and Laura!

Greatest thanks to Lisa Allen for the guiding advice, to Susan Morse for the proofreading prowess, to Miranda S. Hewlett for the Judaic editorial proficiency, to Ugly Shyla for the Hoodoo mojo.

Vibrational gratitude to Jerry Abstract, Sopor Aeternus (Anna-Varney Cantodea), and Monica Richards for the "musickal" soundscapes throughout. Additional gratitude to Catherine Lee Cunningham and Stephañaya Tyler for facilitating the book's mind-blowing "red right handed" synchronicity!

Additional thanks to the brilliant Elysia Gallo and the fine folks at Llewellyn for the encouragement, meticulous editorial precision, and creative expertise. This book has become something far more powerful and beautiful than I had originally envisioned. Thanks as well to Melanie Marquis for the book's initial inspiration!

Blessed be to my friends, family, and readers alike—you,

and my little guy Catskills, help me stay focused on the light in a world brimming with darkness.

God(s) bless. Om shanti shanti shanti,

Raven Digitalis
Samhain, 2025

Contents

Section IV: Otherwise Shadow Spells

144 Shadow Spells, Charms & Rituals

Shadow Reflections

Introduction

Greetings and blessings! I am very happy you're here. Because our time on earth is valuable and time is really all we have, it's an honor that you've chosen to spend some of it with me. This spellbook is designed to be a convenient and practical reference for those who prefer to work magick by way of shadow.

We all have a shadow, and we live in a world of both shadow and light. It's our responsibility to recognize, acknowledge, and work with darker energy for the greater good. Life isn't all love and light, so let's take a step into the shadows to see what work needs to be done. Life is evolution and magick is art.

Although I'm best known for my "empath's trilogy" and "shadow trilogy" (and their accompanying oracle decks), the first spellbook I wrote was published by Llewellyn in 2010: *Planetary Spells & Rituals: Practicing Dark & Light Magick Aligned with the Cosmic Bodies.* It contains spells far more expansive and ritualistic than those found here. What differentiates this book from the aforementioned is the fact that these spells focus specifically on the energy of "shadow," and that the procedures are generally shorter and require fewer materials. Although most of the workings here are relatively simple, they can be incorporated into larger rituals and magickal undertakings.

Shadow Work & This Book

The idea of shadow as it relates to an individual was popularized by Swiss psychologist and metaphysical enthusiast Carl Jung. In addition to archetypes, dreams, synchronicity, and the collective unconscious, Jung explored the concept of the shadow self: the part of everyone's psyche where we find hidden or repressed beliefs, impulses, traumas, inner conflicts, insecurities, and fears. An unrecognized shadow can result in a lifetime of reactivity, pessimism, arrogance, depression, hypersensitivity, narcissism, and other traits that are destructive toward oneself and others.

In Carl Jung's 1951 *Aion: Researches into the Phenomenology of Self*, he writes:

> The shadow is a moral problem that challenges the whole ego-personality, for no one can become conscious of the shadow without considerable moral effort. To become conscious of it involves recognizing the dark aspects of the personality as present and real. This act is the essential condition for any kind of self-knowledge, and it therefore, as a rule, meets with considerable resistance. Indeed, self-knowledge as a psychotherapeutic measure frequently requires much painstaking work extending over a long period.[1]

1. Joseph Campbell, (editor) and R. F. C. Hull (translator), *The Portable Jung* (Viking Penguin, 1971), 145.

It's good to note that in terms of Jung's explorations into the shadow self, this area of the psyche is not regarded as exclusively bad, especially considering that one's untapped greater potential and creativity are part of the shadow self. As for the more so-called negative attributes, we humans have learned to compartmentalize and suppress certain things as part of our evolutionary trajectory for survival and the sake of organization both mentally and emotionally.

Shadow work is beautiful, tough, and necessary. Working with the shadow allows the unseen to become acutely visible.

All forms of shadow magick are best approached when we are actively working with our shadow self and intentionally choosing *not* to deny aspects of the psyche that ordinarily go under the conscious radar. Those of us who perform the tough, honest, vulnerable work of shadow are seekers of self-awareness. Naturally, we are prone to increased sensitivity and challenging beliefs about ourselves and the world. I hope this book provides a bit of padding and reassurance for shadow workers of all varieties.

Shamanically speaking (for lack of a better term), the variety of shadow work found here is actually lightwork in disguise—although I'd personally never go as far as to call myself a lightworker! The greatest, most genuinely powerful light can be discovered by actively and honestly working with shadow for the greater good.

In his groundbreaking book *Out of the Shadows: An Exploration of Dark Paganism & Magick*, John J. Coughlin writes:

> It is important to remember that focusing only on the darker side is just as dangerous as focusing only on the lighter side. Balance is important, and even though some may relate to one aspect more than the other, we must always remain open to the other aspects. Life consists of the interplay of these opposites that naturally complement each other.[2]

I would be remiss to say that there's nothing to fear in the shadows; it can be frightening terrain, whether it's taking a walk through a moonlit forest or metaphysically walking through the recesses of repressed trauma. In its innumerable forms and interpretations, the force of shadow upholds our reality.

All the spells, charms, procedures, recipes, dedications, ceremonies, and workings in this book relate to shadow in one form or another. Because *internal* shadow work is foundational, it serves as the book's opening theme, setting the stage for other forms of shadow work.

Section I most predominately explores shadow in a Jungian context. It is purely focused on inner work and the process of meeting and working with aspects our shadow selves for the purpose of healing and personal evolution. Themes of self-awareness, the unconscious mind, and healing through struggle permeate the opening section.

Section II invites readers to reflect on their interaction with the outside world; that which is separate from oneself. Although we are all interconnected and truly one, our souls are here in this lifetime experiencing a division from the whole—or so it appears.

---

2. John J. Coughlin, *Out of the Shadows: An Exploration of Dark Paganism & Magick* (Waning Moon Publications / 1stBooks Library, 2001), 10.

We have different bodies, minds, and experiences separate from each other's, but we are truly pieces of a fractured singularity. The spells and workings in the second section encompass powerful methods of protection, cleansing external energetic accumulation, and interacting with the shadow of society.

Section III shifts our focus to the natural world. Nature is a dance of darkness and light, so it's only appropriate for us to examine and explore the shadow of reality expressed by Mother Nature. The third section's spells and procedures include working with the dark moon and eclipses, harnessing the energy of naturally occurring liminal spaces, and utilizing shadow-related ritual tools and magickal components.

Section IV exclusively relates to the unseen world. The energy of shadow not only relates to the unseen or hidden aspects of ourselves, but also to the oft' invisible realms with which we're connected. The workings found in the final section focus on the astral plane, the realm of spirits and ancestors, and the realm of sleep and dreaming.

Right before the bibliography (which doubles as a suggested reading list for all intents and purposes) is a list of correspondences. This list is meant to act as an easy point of reference when performing a spell or ritual related to shadow work. Categorized by spiritual intention, the components listed under any given subject include herbs, trees, stones, minerals, curios, and unconventional items aligned to various purposes. Many of these can act as substitutes if you lack a suggested ingredient in a spell; just look up its purpose in this section and fine-tune your ritual from there.

Categorizing some of the procedures proved challenging because many could easily be placed in multiple chapters. Shadowy energy is largely interpretative, so don't be surprised to see a few unexpected entries here and there! Luckily, I believe they've all come together exactly as they were meant to, and I hope you find them inspirational.

Artists, mystics, and creative types often reference receiving vision or inspiration, whether attributed to the Muses, higher consciousness, or another invisible force. This process in itself is related to shadow work because of its connection to the unconscious.

This book was destined to have exactly 144 workings, a number that appeared repeatedly in my mind when sitting with the manuscript's energetic presence. My best guess for this is because 12 by 12 is the number of zodiac signs multiplied by itself. Twelve is also the number of chapters in the book! Additionally, 1 + 4 + 4 = 9, the number associated with Yesod on esoteric Qabalah's Tree of Life. Yesod is ruled by Moon as a planetary body, which is directly tied to shadow work and the unconscious. As a unit of measurement, 12 dozen (122) is called a *gross*, but I assure you that only a handful of these spells are icky.

I am pleased to say that this book includes a lucky number of seven spells written by guest authors. These workings are written by friends of mine who are experienced in shadow work and various systems of Witchcraft. Their excellent pieces benefit this book's objective, and I hope you find them helpful. Just like the total of 144 workings, the number seven continued to appear to me as the exact number of guest spells this book wanted, so to speak, and it came together seamlessly. May they serve you well.

You'll also discover Shadow Reflections throughout, eight in total (two per section) and related to each section in which they fall. These reflections are also relevant to shadow workers in a general sense. I felt it important to highlight these bits of information and contemplation so that readers can keep these points in mind when performing shadow magick. You are likely to discover that some of these reflections provide new food for thought, while others serve as good reminders for what you already know. We all need refreshers from time to time, and those "oh yeah!" moments can go a long way.

Keep in mind that it doesn't really matter what you call yourself. Most readers will identify as Witches or occultists, but that won't be the case for everyone. Spellcraft and shadow work can beneficial for spiritual seekers of all varieties, traditions, and labels.

This is a judgment-free zone. Whoever you are and whatever your background, you're valued. You deserve to incorporate shadow work in your practice for deeper healing, protection, and connection to the unseen. Whether you're an experienced practitioner or a magickal neophyte, you'll find something here to enrich your path. Use critical thinking, contemplation, and intuition to determine when to perform any given spell, and consider how you might customize workings to fit your practice.

Shadow work is an expansive subject, and a small book like this is not designed to delve deeply into academic theories. Instead, the work here is practical and can accompany your own research into psychological and metaphysical definitions of shadow.

Some of the subjects and themes touched upon here are quite serious. However, this little collection of workings is not meant to trivialize or commodify shadow work in any way. In the grander scope and importance of shadow work, this book is designed to act as an addendum or tool along the way for seekers who called toward spiritual heavy lifting.

If you're curious to delve deeper into shadow work in a magickal and metaphysical context, I suggest my book *A Witch's Shadow Magick Compendium* alongside Kate Freuler's *Of Blood & Bones: Working with Shadow Magick & the Dark Moon* (see the bibliography for publishing information about these titles).

I am fully aware that some folks will pick up this book hoping to find cursing techniques, baneful spells, maledictions, demonic summoning, and edgy, disturbing rituals to gain power over others. While such things *do* fall under the category of shadow work, the spells found here are firmly rooted in ethical practice. As a spiritual writer, I would be foolish to karmically entwine myself with unknown others' affairs by providing ammunition. Instead, cursing alternatives are judiciously offered, and a number of highly protective spells can be found in chapter 4. Relatedly, there is no "black magick" in this book. Although magick is a rainbow-hued tool that is never actually black or white, the term black magick is well-known, implying harmful, manipulative, coercive, controlling, and predatory magickal work. For the sake of definition, black magick can be viewed as magick that purposefully violates another's free will for the purpose of the caster's personal gain. Yawn! Causing destruction in order to feel high and mighty? That's some daft, insecure shit.

While there are rare instances where such magick works for the greater good, other books cover these subjects in more depth. The shadow work encouraged in this humble spellbook is expressly for the purpose of influencing change for the better. There's enough suffering in the world. I think that in the vast majority of cases, performing so-called black magick is unnecessary, unsophisticated, and spiritually juvenile. I'm more a fan of increasing empowerment than gaining power.

I won't deny that there are many cultures and traditions around the globe who have and do practice the deepest, most horrific acts of magick using tortured animals, human corpses, and living people who are kidnapped and enslaved for organ harvesting—all for superstitious and alleged magickal use. This soul-shaking depravity is happening right now in the world we live in. It's good to be aware of this evil and approach our magick with morals and maturity. We are meant inspire the world toward becoming a better place, not to be part of the problem.

Approaching the Spells

The spells in this book are quite diverse, but all fall under the category of shadow magick. Shadow work can, at times, be overwhelming and unpleasant. Inner work in particular requires *courage*, *vulnerability*, and utmost *self-awareness*. These three qualities are one's best allies when facing, processing, and internally alchemizing emotions that beg attention.

In many ways, shadow work is all about interacting with the subconscious, the unconscious, and the obscured. Shadow work is beautiful, tough, and necessary. Working with the shadow allows the unseen to become acutely visible.

As you work up to casting one of these spells, ground and center your energy however it works best for you and enter a light meditative state. Ceremony should be something special and sacred. It's up to you how many bells and whistles you'd like to attach to any given ritual, as everyone will vibe differently with everything offered here. Be mindful of your ceremonial callings, needs, and preferences.

Successful spellcraft should be approached from a *somewhat altered or non-ordinary state of consciousness*. A mystical mindset helps shift energy within and without, making spellcraft something special, significant, and out of the ordinary. Your conscious awareness should be shifted, calmed, and attuned to the magickal work at hand. It's important to be in a certain state of mind to perform effective magick. Although some natural drugs can be tremendous allies for inducing a shift in conscious awareness, they aren't the *only* way to reach a lightly altered, spell-appropriate state. Other methods include breathwork, meditation, dance, movement, mantras, chanting, and music. Everyone's methods of reaching a mystical state of consciousness are different and don't always need to include a lot of performance. Sometimes a slight brainwave shift is all it takes to enter a state of focus. Don't doubt yourself or your magick. Confidence is key!

The success of mystical and magickal work relies on the caster's mental and emotional state at any given time, so ensure that you're in a proper headspace before casting. Before performing a spell, give it some good thought. Also ensure that you're in a quiet, safe place when working magick whether it's at your altar, in a room devoted to rituals, or a serene location in nature.

Casting a circle before spellcasting can add a major level of importance and potency to magickal work. The case of whether to cast a circle for any particular spell is entirely dependent on the individual's practice and the purpose of the spell or ritual.

You can choose to cast a circle and call the quarters/quadrants/watchtowers for any of these spells or not—it's totally up to you!

Each spell assumes that the caster has their own ritualistic method of "setting the space" before performing spellcraft. If this isn't the case for you, that's okay; just make sure you're in comfortable, private space that's been energetically cleansed beforehand through visualization, smoke cleansing, instruments, affirmations, or whatever is most comfortable. Do what feels right.

The shadow work encouraged in this humble spellbook is expressly for the purpose of influencing change for the better. There's enough suffering in the world.

Consider any given spell and how it could best suit your needs based on your personal knowledge and practice. Some readers may methodically align their workings with astrological shifts, planetary hours, and cosmic alignments. Other readers will feel more comfortable calling upon their guides, gods, guardians, spirit animals, the angelic realm, the ancestors, and so on. Everyone is different, and that's the beauty of magickal work, including prayer: It is accessible, personal, and very much our birthright!

The biggest pointer I can offer is *don't overthink your spells*. Our craft is one of wisdom and knowledge mixed with intuition and creativity. Magick is an art for a reason, and what is art but *creative*? While many of the world's spells, such as those from ancient tomes and grimoires read more like precise recipes and exacting procedures (and are likely best performed as such), spellcraft in the realm of Neopagan Witchcraft encourages intuitive modification.

Tailor these spells to fit you personally. Don't do them precisely by the book; add your own spin, fine-tune words or ingredients, or modify something that just doesn't feel right. There's no need to perform these spells down to the letter—seriously! Feel free to modify these spells in any way you see fit. When spellcraft is personally refined, the magick flows with power and ease.

Ingredients, Substitutions & Ethics

The wise magickal practitioner is aware of how their life choices affect others' lives and the world at large. Everything we do is significant, and that includes the ingredients and components we use in spellcraft.

Purchase supplies at your local metaphysical supplier if possible. Independent botanicas and herbal supply shops are also excellent to support, as are a number of small businesses on Etsy, eBay, and small online webstores. Let's support our hardworking visionary comrades!

If you harvest herbs or other spellcasting components, do so with mindfulness and reverence, leaving offerings and taking only what you need. Don't destroy a plant or damage a cozy critter's home! We can work gently with the ecosystem.

Similarly, from feathers to bones, if you're using animal parts in a spell, know their source and ensure that your use hasn't contributed to an animal's suffering. Even seemingly small choices are significant, such as using a free-range "happy chicken" egg instead of a factory-farmed one or using an insect's carcass you've discovered instead of killing a bug for a spell. Everything, including that which we consume physically and environmentally, carries an imprint and creates an impact.

When it comes to gemstones, I encourage you to use your own moral compass. Many of these spells call for gemstones of various types, as these associations are traditional. As before, it's a good idea to modify these spells to fit your specific circumstances, supplies, and inclinations. Unless a gemstone's source is explicitly stated by a retailer, it's hard to know if it was mined under inhumane working conditions. Numerous mining operations for natural materials are deplorably exploitative. It's therefore best to either simply use the gemstones you already have instead of buying new ones or, if you do buy new ones, limit the quantity and only use what's needed for a spell or energy work. When possible *and* unless a spell requires the stone to be discarded, cleanse and reuse your gemstones. You could also decide to forego the use of gemstones entirely—a totally respectable choice.

Some of these spells offer suggestions for substitutions, but most do not. You may choose to fine-tune a spell based on the ingredients used in a different spell. For example, a spell may call for yarrow for helping with boundaries, but you may instead choose rue for its emphasis on energetic protection, having noticed that a different spell mentions this quality.

Regarding herbal substitutions, you may wish to consider the genetics and vibration of the plant suggested. Ideal substitutions are herbs of the same *family*, such as using ginger instead of galangal, or lemon verbena instead of vervain. Another way to substitute is to use a plant that has similar *qualities* to the one suggested. For example, if you can't find the renowned herb hyssop for a curse-removal bath, you may choose to substitute something else similarly renowned for removing curses, such as thistle, rue, or poke root.

An example of a common substitution is frankincense versus rosemary; the two are unrelated but are sometimes interchanged due to the similar smell they produce when burned, and the fact that both have qualities of cleansing and raising vibrations. Another example is American mandrake, actually called mayapple, which is a frequent substitute for authentic mandrake root; the two are unrelated but have similar energetic signatures.

When in doubt about substitutions, perform divination, such as scrying, tarot, or using a pendulum to determine if something can serve as a suitable substitute for any given ingredient or component.

If you use sage for cleansing, please explicitly know your source. Indigenous-sourced sage is by far the best choice, as it supports independent sellers and marginalized communities—an act of wisdom. As a number of Native American friends have advised me, avoid using or purchasing Californian *white sage* specifically *unless* it's been explicitly ethically sourced. The vast majority of white sage on the market has been poached from protected lands by folks who don't mind harming an ecosystem and breaking laws for financial gain. Let's not give poachers one ounce of business.

In the case of oils, I highly suggest only using *essential* oils. Fragrant oils are chemical concoctions; although scent of any type aids in the sensory experience of magickal work, the purer an ingredient, the better. Chemicals *out*, Mama Nature *in*! The same can be said for incense. Most stick incense contains chemical fragrance, so selecting high-quality incense sticks or resin is the best choice. If choosing sticks, I have found that Indian and Japanese incense tends to be the most pure and natural, and there are a handful of joss stick producers in the West who specialize in sourcing and compounding authentic ingredients, including Fred Soll's "resin on a stick" blends (the only dragon's blood stick I'll use!)—it's worth a slightly higher price tag and supports fellow good-doers.

Crafty Pointers

Here are a few points worth considering when approaching spellcraft in general.

- Working with deities, spirit guides, ancestors, saints, or familiar spirits is optional when performing a spell; just be sure to respect them and form a relationship rather than "using" them like an object at your every beck and call. To do so would be a dangerous transactional demand rather than a relationship of mutual respect.
- Be mindful of astrological influences for spells, most importantly the Sun (the most influential) followed by the Moon. If it's your practice, use current astrological information to determine the best time to perform certain spells. When in doubt, trust your intuition.
- When spellcasting, attune to and enchant each ingredient as you see fit. The most basic and successful way of doing

so is to meditate with each herb, stone, candle, or component, visualizing its essence awakening and surrounded with the energy of your intention.

- Incense resin and the burning of herbs generally require quick-light (self-igniting) charcoal tablets and a safe mini-cauldron or dish to hold the smoldering charcoal atop sand. These charcoals are available at metaphysical supply stores, Catholic supply shops, online retailers, and smoke shops that sell hookahs and shisha (hookah tobacco). Do not light an incense charcoal indoors: The quick-igniting process requires the coal to be compounded with foul-smelling components whose energy is known to banish and chase out energies of all varieties, such as sulfur, saltpeter, and gunpowder. Additionally, if you aren't allowed to use flame or incense in your current living situation, spritzes and sprays are fabulous substitutes.
- I do not advise lighting candles with matches unless you do so away from your spiritual workspace, as the smoke from the head's sulfur chases away energies. However, lighting matches is advisable if you're performing a ritual to banish harmful forces in a space; you'll see this recommended later for specific rituals and spells.
- Know what you're working with both in terms of your own constitution as well as the materials you've chosen. This is especially the case when ingesting anything, like a tea or tincture suggested in a spell. If you're on antidepressants, benzodiazepines, antipsychotics, opiates, or anything that works with your brain chemistry, be aware of herbal interactions and contraindications. For example, St. John's wort and skullcap don't mix with SSRIs. For more information, please refer to this book's disclaimer.

Notes About These Shadow Spells

Before jumping into this particular spellbook, allow me to answer some potential FAQs straight away.

- A handful of spells found here are more similar to rituals, meditations, recipes, or dedications, even if I sometimes refer to them all as spells for simplicity's sake. Either way, they're all magickal and designed for positive transformation within and without.
- The ingredients and components suggested in these spells are directly influenced by both historic and modern magickal use of plants, stones, minerals, animal bits, curios, and other items spanning numerous cultures and periods of time. Any given spell suggests the most potent and renowned ingredients I could discover for each spell's particular purpose.
- Note that these spells are designed for individuals in the Northern Hemisphere. Readers in the Southern Hemisphere may need to adapt things here and there, namely some of the sabbat information and details about casting energy in a *deosil* (clockwise) or *widdershins* (counterclockwise/anticlockwise) direction.
- Most of the spoken words in these spells rhyme, but some do not. As always, feel free to modify certain words or anything else to more personally suit your approach.
- Some practitioners believe that spellcraft can only affect the self and has no effect on other individuals or external entities. This psychospiritual viewpoint is perfectly valid,

and for those who hold these views, section I will resonate most significantly.

- You may wish to modify some of these spells to become *silent* rituals. Silence connects to shadow in the sense that it does away with expressive vocalization and instead brings a unique sense of focus to the work at hand. Alternatively, you may choose to ritualize a spell in total silence *except for* its spoken words of power.
- Unless otherwise advised, it's a good choice to face west for many of these workings; this is the direction of the setting sun and the realm of emotion, empathy, and shadow work.
- I do not give a list of ingredients or supplies before explaining each spell, charm, or ritual; these are instead mentioned throughout each procedure. Please fully read through, study, and reflect on any given spell before performing it. Keep a notecard or notebook handy to ensure that you have all the ingredients and tools you need, and feel free to track your performed rituals and progressions in a dedicated journal.
- I also offer personally customized spell kits and spellcraft advice, in addition to professional tarot readings through my website, www.ravendigitalis.com. Please reach out any time for advice or spiritual services. I love keeping in touch and I love being of service!

Section I

Internal Shadow Spells

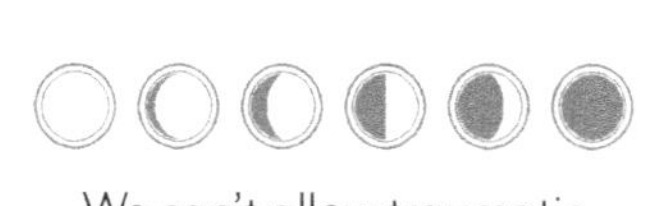

We can't allow traumatic imprints to shape our lives. It takes bravery and self-awareness to overcome horrible and saddening experiences and, in many ways, will always bear those scars. And still, we must carry on.

Shadow Reflection: The Work of a Lifetime

Internal shadow work is a lifelong process and not something to approach flippantly. Most importantly, the work does not need to be done all by yourself. You are not alone!

Shadow work, especially that which is focused internally, can be emotionally triggering. It begs for unresolved traumas and repressed emotions to tumble into the light for the purpose of recognizing, healing, and inspiring personal growth. The difficult work can benefit every aspect of our lives and also uplifts those around us in return.

Asking for help and soliciting assistance is of utmost importance for gaining perspective and learning lifelong skills. Whether it's therapy, counseling, psychiatric care, or trusted friends and family, we are all here to support each other in life's crazy adventure.

Shadow Reflection: Hope & Expectation

We deserve to condition ourselves to expect the good. Everything we do and think is an act of *karma*, the word itself translating as "action" or "deed," that leaves behind a resulting potency that connects to cause and consequence.[3]

Shadow workers are often highly sensitive, psychic, or empathic. We experience life's ups, downs, and all-arounds, and it's our job to keep these things in check. We must place our health first, physically, mentally, and emotionally.

Hopefulness helps us sow beneficial karmic seeds for ourselves and others. Still, we must remain consistently realistic in life, especially during those times when our inner dialogue is self-defeating and when the world around us feels threatening.

Quite often, our negative and positive outlooks and expectations become self-fulfilling prophecies. Don't fall into the hole of hopelessness in your personal life or about your country or society; do something, anything, whatever you can, as often as you are able, to help make the world a more loving place starting with yourself. We don't only work with our *own* shadows—we work with the world's. We and no one else get to determine our happiness.

3. John A. Grimes, "Karma" in *A Concise Dictionary of Indian Philosophy* (SUNY Press, 1999), 160–62.

CHAPTER 1

Spells Concerning the Past

As any magickal practitioner worth their salt agrees, shadow work of all varieties begins with the personal shadow. This process is very much an ongoing work that lasts a lifetime and looks different for everyone. We each carry our own versions of insecurity, fear, and emotional trauma.

The spells in this chapter deal with internal shadow magick that focuses on the past. Painful imprints of the past can easily lead to depression, pessimism, emotional burnout, and low self-esteem. These spells target such imprints and many of the emotions and beliefs that can arise from emotionally jarring experiences.

There are times when the shadow protects us by compartmentalizing emotional responses to difficult experiences. However, these imprints remain with us just under the surface and can negatively affect our daily lives. We must seek internal resolution in order to healthfully and wisely forge ahead.

You should by no means feel as though you need to work through every spell in this chapter or any other. We all need different medicine at different times. It's also important to remember the saying "the only way out is through." Actively working with challenges from the past is a way of saying "I refuse to regress and I refuse to repress!" When we examine and work with the past at our own pace and with a sense of honesty, we encourage those shadowy aspects to resolve, helping us become more whole and more healed.

Invoking Self-Forgiveness

Day-to-day life is heavy when we carry the weight of the past on our shoulders. Anxiety, depression, and physical health issues are given room to manifest if we're constantly ruminating about the past or feel as though we're defined by our mistakes and negative experiences.

This spell urges the caster to exercise forgiveness for past mistakes and shortcomings. Regret is a natural part of the human experience, and the mere ability to *have* regret means that not are you able to feel but you have already evolved into a wiser, more self-aware individual who is unlikely to fall back into similar negative behavioral cycles. This spell is best performed at nighttime and during the dark moon, but these conditions are not required.

In a sacred space, safely burn the herbs lavender and/or hyssop atop an incense charcoal while entering a meditative state. Focus on your regrets, putting yourself back in those moments in time. Feelings of embarrassment may rise, and you're likely to think, "I should have done or said this differently." While that may be true, the past remains in the past, and it's time to move on.

While the herbal smoke surrounds you, communicate to yourself in each past scenario. Allow yourself to cry if needed, and acknowledge whatever emotions arise. Tell your former self that you've evolved, changed, and learned from those mistakes. Tell them that you understand their reasons for doing or saying what they did and that things will get better in the future. Now that you've learned and changed, extend empathy to your former self by communicating with them in each regrettable scenario, visualizing them bathed in blue and white healing light.

Once you feel the working is complete, take a warm cleansing bath or shower with a bundle of fresh sagebrush, if possible. Otherwise, use a separate sachet and squeeze the herb's energy on your body as a watery elixir. The energy of sagebrush is said to specifically work for self-forgiveness and easing life's regrets. If this is unattainable, consider a sage bundle or essential oil, but try to steer clear of white sage (see page 11 under "Ingredients, Substitutions & Ethics" on why).

The following morning, collect the ashes of the herbs and mix them in a pouch with sea salt. Consider adding the stone rhodonite and/or rose quartz, both of which are said to aid in the process of forgiveness and the invocation of unconditional love. Keep this mixture at your bedside and speak regrets into the bag any time they continue to arise, knowing that your future is brighter as a result of making amends with shortcomings of the past.

Mending Past Wounds

We all have physical and emotional scars. However, we can choose to disallow experiences from the past to determine our future. This spell uses sympathetic magick ("this represents that") and is best performed in conjunction with regular work aimed at resolving prior challenges, be it therapy, supportive friends, or a daily meditation regimen.

Shadow work centered around emotional trauma, learned behaviors, and psychological conditioning can be challenging and uncomfortable. It is only with practice and support that true healing begins to emerge piece by piece. To quote Timothy Roderick's classic text *Dark Moon Mysteries: Wisdom, Power and Magic of the Shadow World:*

> The shadow is the emotional part of you that you either don't want to look at or cannot look at. When you are forced into confronting it you feel uncomfortable, yet it is an essential part of human makeup. You wouldn't be human without a shadow.[4]

For this spell, you'll want to procure a 12 × 12" sheet of leather, be it cowhide used for leathercraft, deerskin from a hunt, or a vegan leather alternative.

In a sacred space without disturbance, make yourself comfortable. Light a red candle and some all-natural incense. Put on relaxing instrumental or downtempo electronic music if you find it helpful.

Pay attention to your breath, becoming keenly aware of your body and mind. When you feel a sense of mystical alignment, call forth your guides:

Beloved guardians on the Inner Planes,
I implore your assistance here and now.
Please aid in healing my wounds,
That I may become whole again!

---

4. Timothy Roderick, *Dark Moon Mysteries: Wisdom, Power and Magic of the Shadow World* (Llewellyn Publications, 2016), 15.

Using your athame or another sharp blade, carefully cut a series of slashes in the hide while thinking about your wounds. Take your time and allow emotions to arise naturally.

Once you've put your wounds to form, speak the call to your guides once again. Stitch up each wound using a needle and thread of your choice. (You may need a leathercraft needle for this purpose.) Cover each stitched-up wound with pure honey and, once finished, roll it up like a scroll, tie it shut with the same thread you used for stitching, and keep it in a secret place. Give thanks to your guides in your own words.

Continue to pay attention in daily life; you are likely to notice emotional triggers when they arise. When they do, recall the spell and choose a new internal response. Over time, your inner ability to mindfully respond rather than react will become second nature.

After three lunar cycles (or simply when intuition guides you) find a secret place off-property to bury the hide and lay it to rest. If the hide you used is not leather, "bury" it in a biodegradable bag with soil and toss it in the trash to be landfilled. Thank your guides and recognize your achievement.

Processing Traumatic Experiences

Unfortunately, the experience of trauma is a part of life to one degree or another. Trauma occurs in varying levels in different people, and we all have unique ways of processing and/or repressing memories and feelings associated with these occurrences. While therapy and medication (herbal or allopathic) are two of the best remedies for PTSD, a little magick can also be of benefit.

We can't allow traumatic imprints to shape our lives. We are not broken. Just as the body itself can heal its injuries with proper care and attention, so can the unseen bodies of mind and emotion. It takes bravery and self-awareness to overcome horrible and saddening experiences; in many ways, we will always bear those scars. And still, we must carry on. We can't lose hope; life doesn't have to feel perpetually lackluster or frightening. Although it takes years of work that we are all very much capable of, this simple spell can aid in the healing process. It can be performed as often as needed and whenever intuition guides.

This meditative spell helps begin or reinforce the process of healing from traumatic occurrences. Perform any additional work you wish that feels rebirthing, refreshing, and renewing. Continue any real-world work to disallow trauma from taking control over the happy and healthy life you deserve.

If possible, procure or create a necklace strand of rowan berries. Also called witch wood and mountain ash, the rowan tree's gorgeous ruby berries are ripe in the autumn in the Western Hemisphere. If you're unable to procure rowan, simply wear a beaded necklace or *mala* (Buddhist or Hindu prayer beads), or better yet, wear both!

For added focus, begin by running each of the mala's 108 beads through your fingers similar to a rosary, while chanting words of power that feel right to you. When in doubt, chant the Sanskrit word *om*.

In a dark and quiet space, light a gray candle and some nice incense. If you don't have a gray candle, you can use one black and one white candle, or one black and one red. Sit in solemnity with a fresh pomegranate. Cut the fruit and eat some of the juicy seeds. Between mouthfuls, repeat the following as many times as you see fit:

In the past I've been wounded,
In the past I've been scorned.
I forbid those pains from returning,
For I now am reborn!

Offer the remainder of the fruit outdoors afterward and take a cleansing bath or shower to seal the spell.

Generational Trauma Healing

We all carry generational imprints, and many of these are written into our DNA. Like the deer whose offspring somehow know to avoid traffic, genetic memories often manifest in the form of instinct. Biology considered, generational trauma can also revolve around the conditioning of one's upbringing, such as a parent's unresolved trauma being projected on the child. These behaviors and imprints can go back countless generations. Concepts such as family curses also fall under this category. Additionally, the idea of traumatic imprints from past lives cannot be overlooked.

Perform this spell alongside any additional workings aimed at nullifying generational, familial, ancestral, and past life trauma, regardless of its source. We have the power, awareness, and responsibility to break traumas and conditioning that once seemed beyond our control. If you are more curious about this fascinating topic, I encourage you to research epigenetics.

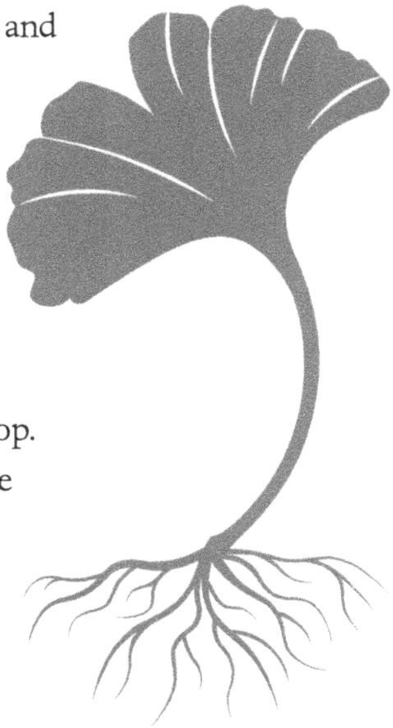

This spell uses ginkgo—to incorporate it, you could burn a leaf, sip ginkgo biloba tea, or purchase a ginkgo energy shot from a Chinese Medicine shop. The reason for tapping into ginkgo is the fact that it's the oldest living tree in the world and therefore carries associations with the distant past and the power of resilience.

Additionally, incorporate any type of dried mushroom. The mycelium network is the most ancient life-producing entity here on Earth; the fungus among us is in fact the foundation of life itself. And speaking of resilience, mycelia (of which mushrooms are the fruiting body) are even capable of consuming stones and rocks over time, allowing life to flourish where it was otherwise barren.

In a pinch, if you're not able to procure ginkgo or a 'shroom, simply gaze at a photo of the ginkgo tree and another of a mushroom, consciously calling upon their ancient presence.

On a fresh sheet of paper (ideally parchment), draw the symbol on the previous page, which represents both ginkgo and mycelium, along with the phrase "generational trauma." These words can be written either inside or somewhere around the symbol. Include any additional words, symbols, and sigils aimed at what you're breaking. This paper can later be buried, burned, or discarded. Your drawing doesn't have to be perfect; it just needs to carry your intention of linking these powerful forces.

After connecting to ginkgo and mycelium, focus strongly on the manifestations of generational trauma you have endured or are currently facing. Forcefully tear the paper four times, proclaiming the following with each rip:

These imprints aren't mine,
This pain must unwind;
This trauma through time,
I hereby unbind!

Consoling the Inner Child

We all have the psychospiritual ability to communicate with our inner child and with other pieces of ourselves from the past who may have sustained injury or trauma. Numerous modern approaches to psychotherapy encourage a person to communicate with parts of themselves that endured difficult experience, such as with psychotherapy's Internal Family Systems (IFS) approach. This practice can be seen as a less intense relative to the core-shamanic practice of soul retrieval, where one reintegrates fractured pieces of their spirit in deep meditation.

Give attention to the part of your past you wish to work with, such as the child who was betrayed by an adult, or the teenager who fell in with the wrong crowd. Repeat this working whenever you wish (the dark moon is ideal), bringing to mind a different aspect of yourself each time. For our purposes, we will work with one piece of the self at a time. Don't hesitate to continue working with one specific part on a number of occasions—the healing process takes time and effort.

During this working, carry or wear a piece of bloodstone and drink a cup of tea that contains valerian root or rosemary. Light a blue, indigo, or violet candle for healing. If possible, get a photo of yourself or your belongings from around the time of the spiritual fracture. In a quiet, safe, meditative place, call upon your lifelong spirit guides and guardians. Perform any protective or cleansing magick that feels appropriate.

See yourself at that time in your life, bringing the image of your former self to your mind's eye. In your own words, communicate with that younger self who stands before you. They are likely to appear wounded or frightened. Tell them that they have every right to feel how they're feeling and that you're sorry they're hurting. Explain that you are their future self and that life will get happier, easier, and safer with time. Assume the role of a big sibling, encouraging them to keep their head up and to realize that things will get better.

Take as much time as you need to feel any emotions you need to experience and communicate what you believe is important for them to hear. Conclude by visualizing both your past and present selves smiling and surrounded with swirling blue, violet, and white light as you feel a renewed sense of confidence and trust in the process of this lifetime.

Reversing Bad Luck

When it seems like life is one big series of unfortunate events, the universe is trying to say something. Instead of getting discouraged or distraught, take a step back and pay attention. If you've experienced a string of what feels like bad luck, higher Powers That Be are encouraging you to change your focus, saying that you're offtrack in some way. And much of what feels like a string of misfortune really has to do with perspective: If you've been experiencing difficult things and are therefore *expecting* the worst, you're bound to attract such experiences in big ways and small. A general shift in focus fueled by a daily gratitude attitude is a highly effective remedy.

Bad luck and repetitive letdowns can be aggravating, frustrating, and discouraging. This energy can easily snowball if one continues to anticipate the worst, wait for the other shoe to drop, and feel like there's always a catch to anything positive.

Truth be told, placing negative preconditions (preconceived notions) on reality goes against the natural evolutionary flow of individual and collective progression, as we are constantly evolving toward greater success both personally and collectively. Use this spell to help bring in the good luck while you actively work against negative beliefs in daily life.

For this spell, you'll need to light a black candle and a red candle. Small chime candles are perfectly suitable. On the black candle, carve an arrow pointing downward. On the red, inscribe an arrow pointing upward.

Between the candles, place a lucky hand root in a small bowl on top of the herbs bayberry, vervain, feverfew, and/or vetiver (vetivert). Alternatively, simply anoint a lucky hand root with essential oil of vetiver. Both feverfew and vetiver are said to transform bad luck into good, and they're the two most important components to the spell. You may also wish to incorporate aventurine in some manner, as it is considered a stone of luck. If lucky hand root is difficult to acquire, anoint the piece of aventurine in its place.

Focused intently on the root, stone, and/or herbs now illuminated by candlelight, proclaim the following three times, first in a whisper, second in regular speech, and third in a loud voice:

O Fortuna, O Fortuna, O Fortuna!
Bad luck begone,
All difficulty reverse!
I am free from misfortune,
I'm released from this curse!
O Fortuna, O Fortuna, O Fortuna!

After the candles have burned down, mix any remaining wax with the root, stone, and herbs. Keep this mixture in a small drawstring sachet to carry on your person or hang above your front doorframe.

Releasing Bitterness

Disappointments from the past, especially if they've been ongoing, are prone to influencing pessimism in daily life. This spell targets bitterness resulting from life's harshness and hardships. While it's easy to lose faith in the prospect of good things happening in life, the future remains undetermined. Even if we've had it rough, we can actively choose not to lose hope in life, humanity, and ourselves. Even though they seem unavoidable, feelings of hopelessness and nihilism are in fact choices.

Simply recognizing dissatisfaction in life as molded by experiences of the past is enough to influence positive change. The next step is to desire positivity and stop expecting the worst. Life's conditioning is strong, but our will is stronger.

Thirteen is a Witchy number signifying the number of lunar cycles in a year. For thirteen minutes, boil water mixed with wormwood in a cauldron or on the stovetop. As you do, gaze at the mixture and state the following thirteen times:

Bitters of wormwood, the harshness of life,
I ask you with reverence to banish my strife.

Allow the mixture to cool and store it in an airtight gallon bag in the freezer. At sunset on a full moon, take the block of ice either to a cemetery crossroads (preferred), to a crossroads on a hiking trail, or to the base of a mighty tree.

Peel away and later discard the plastic bag. Leave the block to melt and, once again, repeat the enchantment thirteen times, concluding by forcefully spitting on the ice. Walk away and return home without looking back.

Energy Despite Burnout

Life can get busy as hell, and there's only so much of us to go around. There's only so much time in the day, and only so much energy we can invest in various responsibilities before tapping into our own precious reserves. Sometimes our energy gets zapped due to life's ongoing demands, the least of which is the upkeep of these bodies we inhabit! Physical and emotional burnout are risks of trying to meet every need and solve every problem all at once.

On one hand, it's admirable and necessary to be productive. We need to accomplish worthwhile things in life. However, if productivity comes at the cost of personal wellness, we run the risk of depleting our energy to the point of crashing. Because all systems are interconnected, burnout can manifest in the form of mental and physical ailment.

It's of great importance to preemptively avoid the crashes of mental and emotional exhaustion. There's not a spell in the world that can take the place of downtime, rest, and self-care. There are times when these necessities are difficult to pencil in, but they really are the most reliable sources of rejuvenation. Life's obligations ebb and flow, and this spell can help promote energy in the face of exhaustion.

The herbs most renowned for inspiring spiritual energy are lotus, yarrow, and angelica root. Make a tea consisting of any or all these herbs to sip before, during, and after the spell. Additionally consider burning myrrh resin, renowned for boosting energy when most needed. The stone citrine is also renowned for helping boost energy levels,

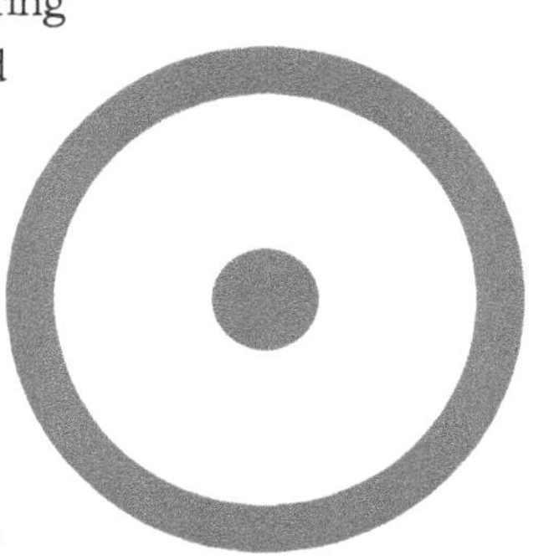

both physically and metaphysically. If procuring these ingredients feels too exhausting, just continue with the rest of the spell.

Purchase a whole, large, plump ginger root at a local farmer's market or grocery store. Peel and cut off a small portion of the ginger root and set it aside for eating later—even a tiny bit will do. Using your athame or small knife, carve the alchemical symbol for the sun (see previous page) into the root six times. In esoteric Qabalah (Kabbalah), six is the number of the Sun, which is ruler of the Tree of Life's luminous sixth sefira, Tiferet (Tiphareth).

Light a yellow candle and stand in front of your altar or in your sacred space. Study the Sun card of the tarot, placing it on your altar to get lost in the imagery while holding the ginger root at your solar plexus. When ready, move your body in ways that invigorate your core or abdomen. Pop the peeled piece of ginger in your mouth and feel its spicy invigoration. While chewing it and moving your abs, say the following six times:

From root to branch, from belly to brain,
Fill me with energy: I need it again!

Keep up the movement for as long as you feel comfortable. Take a deep breath afterward, grounding and centering your energy back into the space.

Keep the ginger root and Sun card on your altar for six days. Afterward, offer the root in a natural area and reincorporate the Sun card back into your deck. Repeat as often as needed and resolve to schedule as much well-deserved downtime as possible!

Relief from Disturbing Sights

Everything we consume affects our minds, bodies, and spirits. Whether it's food, drink, conversation, music, film, social media, or even dreams, life's experiences reverberate and sometimes necessitate focus, lest they turn into traumatic imprints.

This brief spell is ideal for times when you may have inadvertently watched a violent or gory scene in a film or TV show, learned about horrific occurrences on the news, or witnessed something in daily life that left you shaken.

Anoint your eyelids and brow chakra with floral water or something equally pleasant that won't bother the eyes or your skin. Burn the dried leaves of cedar and/or cypress, known to calm the mind and purify negative mental impressions. Taking deep, calming breaths, get the smoke all over your body, especially at the head and heart. Declare the following:

Great gods and guides, what I have seen,
Shakes my core; should not have been.
Lift this disturbance of mind and heart,
So peace prevails within and without.

Shadow-Dancing Grief

Grieving is an ongoing process. We can feel grief about losing family, friends, pets, jobs, our old identities, and really anything else that creates a feeling of loss. We all experience loss in our lives, and these occurrences only increase with time and age.

Grief has no distinct timeline, and there's no ultimate destination in the grieving process aside from acceptance. And even then, acceptance doesn't guarantee the end of pain or sadness, or that episodes of deep emotional processing won't ever pop up again. They most certainly will, and they tend to come in waves.

To help process grief, become acutely aware of your feelings whenever they arise. Those feelings may occur at inconvenient times; if your environment allows, try processing some of this energy through dance.

Begin the ritual by feeling *where* the sadness associated with loss resides within your body when it arises. For many, it's at the heart, head, or stomach area. Place your hands on the area you feel its weight and allow yourself to cry if needed. Become present with the emotion. Once you've tapped into the sensation, dry your tears, wipe your nose, and put on some drumming music. I suggest bookmarking drumming tracks in advance so that you won't have to go digging online with cloudy eyes.

Now move your body slowly at first, increasing in speed. Move your limbs, stretch, pulse your body with the rhythm, and simply surrender to movement. You should be allowing yourself to feel and experience the heavy emotions throughout. There is no wrong way to dance; sacred movement is intuitive and expressive. These energies are being processing in your body and mind. After a while, the feelings will become lighter because your energy will have been activated and dispersed. Exercise also increases endorphins.

While you dance, silently call forth your guides, guardians, or ancestors. Bring to mind who or what you've been in the process of grieving. Continue to move as you pull energy from Mother Earth and Father Sky, allowing it to wash over your body. Send this infinite and comforting energy to what you are grieving. Conclude the ritual by laying on the floor—or, if possible, outside on the grass. Perform any additional prayers and casting of energy from above and below and repeat anytime it is helpful.

CHAPTER 2

Spells Concerning the Present

The spells and workings in this chapter focus on current challenges as they relate to internal shadow work. Inner work does not always need to be focused on the resolution of past experiences. There are times when work we must do is centered in what's happening here and now. This is especially true when we are actively experiencing high amounts of stress that require an immediate response.

This chapter begins with two all-purpose shadow cleansing spells that are both versatile and effective. The chapter then progresses to spells focusing on specific emotions that one may be experiencing at present. Self-criticism, judgment, and sadness are the themes of many of these spells. This is where you'll also find spells aimed at healing experiences related to confusion, anger, stress, isolation, and stagnation. Although many of these challenges can arise from past experiences and conditioning, it's important to address not only the causes but also the symptoms.

Our present selves have been forged by sorrow, loss, and pain ... but *also* by joy, love, and fortitude. If we are able to face our shadows of the past, we are very much capable of facing our shadows of the present.

A Shadow Cleansing Bath

Internal shadow work can be an exhaustive process, and a person certainly gets out what they put in. This ritualistic spell can be utilized when shadow work feels altogether overwhelming.

The water element rules emotion as well as death, release, and workings of shadow. This bath is designed to purify and cleanse, but you can modify by using a shower if a bathtub is unattainable. This is best performed on a Sunday, as it's ruled by the Sun and therefore represents illumination and the light that overcomes darkness.

Plan the morning to ritualize without disturbance. When you wake up, don't speak anything until you utter the spell's spoken words; there is silence in shadow, and shadow in silence. Write these words on a notecard to keep by you in the tub for when you'll verbalize the intentions.

Draw a warm bath while you brew a very strong cup of parsley tea. Strain the herb, take a sip, and add the remaining infusion to the bathwater. Place a piece of rose quartz of any size in the tub. Feel free to add Hoodoo Florida water (or regular floral water) to the bath; otherwise, add a few drops of floral essential oil, such as jasmine, rose, or lavender. Another option is clary sage essential oil, a superpower energetic cleansing component.

As you enter the bath, submerge a dried Rose of Jericho and let it float alongside your body. These "roses" are also called resurrection plants and can be found at most occult stores. When you feel a sense of calm and tranquility, cradle the plant and repeat the following as many times as feels right:

I have been overcome,
but this weight now transforms.
Through all of my struggles,
I am always reborn.

Fully submerge yourself in the warm water a number of times before draining the tub.

So that it has time to unfurl into its unique rosette shape, place the Rose of Jericho on your altar in a bowl of fresh water with a piece of rose quartz, and mark your calendar to remove it the following Sunday. After it dries and curls back up, you can use it again in the same manner whenever the need arises.

Conclude the ritual by getting some direct sunlight, a light snack, and of course a bit of caffeine!

Cleansing by Egg, Feather & Pine

Life requires cleansing and cleaning in mind, body, spirit, environment, and so on. That's just how it goes! If you've felt too much unhelpful shadowy energy or dense vibrations accumulating around you personally, try one of these time-tested methods for removing spiritual blockage.

Use a chicken egg (ideally from a local bird or a company that's humanely certified) to rub your body and aura from top to bottom while visualizing excessive energy entering the vessel. Conclude by throwing this at the base of a tree to be reabsorbed by Mother Earth or, before offering to a tree, break the egg in a clear glass of water to perform divination. Much like in dreams, the symbols that appear in the water will communicate what sort of energies the egg absorbed. This is an Indigenous practice with Mesoamerican roots called *limpia* in Spanish. Egg cleansing has numerous variations and is most commonly associated with Latin American brujería (Witchcraft).

Alternatively or additionally, use a black or partially black feather to brush all over your body from head to toe. Finish by burning the feather outdoors to release what was collected, ideally in the flame of a black candle. As per Hoodoo tradition, feathers from a black hen or rooster are preferred but by no means are required.

You may also roll or brush the branch of a piñon or pine tree all over your body for a similar purpose, also throwing it outdoors or in the trash upon completion.

For added power, burn authentic dragon's blood resin or piñon sap when performing such a cleansing, speaking your own words of power throughout.

Working with Sadness

Sadness is part of existing as a conscious being and is an indication that we are capable of feeling and experiencing life itself. There is no quick fix for sadness, and there's not a spell in the world that's a cure-all. This spell and others similar can, however, become part of the process of working with this particular aspect of the internal shadow.

If sadness is ongoing and perpetual, that's considered depression. While sadness is an emotion (and one of many that depressed people feel, depression itself is a different matter: a mental health condition. If you experience ongoing depression, please seek therapeutic assistance and be open to natural or allopathic medicine.

Consider that you may be experiencing a Dark Night of the Soul. Coined by the mystic Saint John of the Cross, this process of mourning or spiritual emptiness doesn't always have a direct cause. It can last for any amount of time, and most importantly *it does pass.* It is worth researching this experience in depth to comprehend it in detail.

Assuming you're actively working with sadness or depression outside spellcraft alone, this working may be of assistance. Australian priestess Alissandra Moon, owner of Raven Moon Academy describes the experience as such in her book, *Shadow Alchemy: Shadow Work & Spiritual Alchemy for Witches & Lightworkers*:

> The Dark Night is ultimately a sacred purification process that clears away illusions, ego-driven desires, and anything superficial. It creates space for clarity, alignment, and deeper connection with your soul's purpose. This alchemical journey often unfolds in three stages: The breakdown of attachments (Dissolution), facing unresolved pain and shadows (Purification), and emerging renewed and aligned with your higher self (Rebirth). Although painful, the Dark Night is not here to hurt or punish you. It is a divine process designed to free you from what holds you back and prepare you for a more expansive and authentic version of yourself.[5]

Light a yellow candle for uplift, and burn either incense of myrrh to understand sorrow or sandalwood to ease it.

5. Alissandra Moon, *Shadow Alchemy: Shadow Work & Spiritual Alchemy for Witches & Lightworkers* (Raven Moon Academy, 2024), 117.

Blend a sizable herbal mixture of any of the following: weeping willow, borage, rosemary, yew, anise, sage, sunflower, life everlasting, vervain, and Saint John's wort. All these herbs carry qualities of relieving suffering and overcoming sadness.

With the mixture of herbs in front of you at your altar, whisper the following into the herbs six times (six being a solar number) while visualizing them surrounded with a yellow light of inspiration:

By way of plant medicine and the spark of life within,
I choose to be happy through thick and through thin.

Label and store the herbal blend for current and future magickal use, such as using them in the bath, carrying in a sachet, or as a mixture to sprinkle where you see fit. If you wish to more deeply charge or recharge the mixture, do so under sunlight rather than moonlight.

Remediating Stagnation & Melancholy

Everyone experiences moments of ennui from time to time. Life can be challenging and overwhelming, and those moments are clear indications from our bodies and spirits that we need a bit of rejuvenation.

Please keep in mind that although melancholy and gloomy moods are normal and natural at times, they may indicate a depressive disorder when perpetual or ongoing for which professional treatment should be sought.

Because energy levels are likely to be low when seeking a spell like this, take your time in tapping into the abundant energy of the universe. Begin by sitting or lying down and opening your energy to universal light to help shake up the stagnation. With open arms, visualize this light alchemizing the darkness within and around you. Take deep breaths and feel the comforting refreshment.

When ready, call upon your guides and guardians. Hold a piece of weeping willow bark (whether harvested or purchased precut and dried) and channel the remaining stagnant energy into it directly. Use your intuition to determine if you should place the bark on various areas of your body, such as the chakra points. Allow and respectfully instruct the weeping willow's energy to absorb your stagnation and sorrow.

Set aside the willow and replace the energy with one or more of the following herbs, depending on what can assist you best: life everlasting, used for health and strength; motherwort to help with discovering life's purpose; cinquefoil (five-finger grass) to help you discover strengths and accomplish goals; eyebright, an herb that encourages insight into a future path; and white sesame seeds, which can be used to help reveal your greater purpose.

Rub the herb or herbs of choice around your body's energy field, and either eat a little bit of it directly or brew as a tea; this secures the herb's energy inside your body after having done so externally. Speak words of purpose and power while you do so, declaring what you wish to accomplish from place of melancholic stagnation.

When finished, give thanks to your guides and guardians. Complete the working by visiting a flowing body of water—a river or a stream. Throw the willow bark into the water with a resounding "And so it is" or "So mote it be!"

Thriving in the Face of Despair (Guest Spell)

The following spell is written by my friend Thomas Foxglove. Thomas and I met on the ol' interwebs shortly after the release of my first book,

Goth Craft, *in 2007. Because we have a great deal in common, we've naturally kept in touch ever since. Thomas is an eclectic Witch with a passion for poetry as well as LGBTQ+ spirituality and magick. He can be discovered online at www.gaywitch.com.*

Some readers may find themselves wandering an endless night with no moon or stars to guide them, the magick they once knew lying dormant while the weight of stagnation sets in. Music may not resonate anymore, and inspiration might seem like a lost cause. They might struggle to handle their basic needs or simple tasks like getting out of bed or tidying their living space. If this sounds familiar, it *will* get better. Don't give up. You may have to fight and claw your way out of the grave to wake from what feels like a nightmare, but when you do, you will be transformed. In addition to therapy (highly recommended), you can use this spell to level with your shadow.

Begin by setting an altar that you will come back to every evening for seven days. Although not a requirement, the ideal time to begin this seven-day working is seven days before the new moon. Once the new moon arrives, shift your focus to energies of rebirth and renewal.

For this spell, you can use a black seven-day jar candle to represent the shadow or unknown, white for all-purpose, green for healing, or whichever color speaks to you personally. You may alternatively wish to use a seven-knob candle, ensuring that one knob burns each day of the weeklong spell—the choice is entirely your own. Whatever you choose, be certain *not* to light the candle until you reach that point in the spell. Keep in mind that you will light the candle every evening for seven days; each day it should burn either for as long as you feel necessary (in the case of a jar candle) or once a single knob has melted (in the case of a seven-knob candle).

Gather a pen and piece of paper to keep on the altar; you will be using these writing tools throughout the weeklong spell's duration.

Citrine is an ideal stone to use in this spell. You can use it for an energy boost, to light a fire under your heels, to feel the sun's warmth, and to be mindful of shadow traits. If citrine feels too intense or causes an adverse reaction, consider using a more calming crystal such as rose quartz, which is known to boost self-love.

This spell makes use of three small pieces of incense resin: frankincense, myrrh, and dragon's blood. Frankincense can uplift one's vibration, myrrh helps us understand sorrow and lower vibrations, and dragon's blood will both jump-start and amplify the working.

Place the incense pieces on your altar alongside the unlit candle in a holder, the pen, paper, and a disc of incense charcoal. The glowing charcoal should be prepared in a fireproof dish or censer; be sure to ignite the charcoal outdoors beforehand.

Bless and empower all three incense resins by holding them in your hands, closing your eyes, and calling forth the creative forces of the universe, the Divine, patron deities, your ancestors, or whatever feels right for you. Visualize the Divine as a multifaceted diamond. Know and feel the creative forces inside the many faces that manifest as deities and other spiritual forces.

Place the frankincense and myrrh on your altar. Holding only the dragon's blood, say:

I bless this resin from the trees,
To remove all frequencies not best for me.
Dragon's blood I now empower,
In this time and in this hour.
Amplify my spell today,
Speedily, without delay!

Place the piece of dragon's blood on the glowing charcoal, allowing the smoke to fill the space and invigorate your spirit. Pick up the piece of myrrh and say:

Myrrh is next to be imbued.
Let my sorrow be subdued.
And as I work to let it go,
Help me understand my woes.

Place the myrrh to burn on the charcoal. When you're ready, pick up the piece of frankincense and say:

I now empower this frankincense,
To lift me up from harsh past-tense.
Bring me to another level;
Mold me into a righteous rebel.
Free me now from bad vibrations;
Flood my soul with good sensations!

Burn the frankincense and enter a meditative state. See yourself standing in the dark of night, a labyrinth in front of you, damp, cool grass beneath your feet, and a calm wind on your back. Hold your hands over your mind and heart, close your eyes, and take a slow, deep, cleansing breath through the nose and out through the mouth. Repeat this process until you feel relaxed. Visualize bright light illuminating your space, causing your shadow to dance amidst the light show. Feel the light burning away that which is not for your highest good until all that is left is the truth.

Bring to mind those parts of yourself that make you cringe, those wounds that will not close, and your deepest fears. Imagine these things as if they were tangibly before you. See them, feel them, and be aware of their presence.

Now you will face your shadow and ask for closure. Hold the citrine and unlit candle and anoint them with your saliva. Say:

In darkest night and deep despair,
I seek entrance into the lair,
Of the shadow now confined,
To the recesses of my mind.

Envision yourself standing before a labyrinth, lighting a torch. As you do so, light the candle. Continue:

I light this torch right now to see,
The deepest, darkest parts of me,
Help me now to comprehend,
That shadow truly is my friend.

Grab the piece of citrine or stone you've chosen and hold it to your heart. Say:

Reveal the secrets deep within
As I find comfort in my skin.
As the shadows start to dance
I bless this stone now in my trance;
From the morning into night,
Let it be my guiding light.
What once was hidden is plain to see,
My inner child I now set free.
I am reborn with open eyes,
I once was dead, but now I thrive!

Take some time to feel the energy and let your intentions reverberate within and without. Give thanks to those you've called forth and be sure to extinguish the candle if you leave the area or go to bed.

Repeat this working every evening for the next six days. If it's too challenging to schedule the full ritual nightly, opt to perform only the final portion each subsequent night. In this case, you would do away with charging the incense, instead only reinforcing the candle lighting and gemstone procedures.

Carry the citrine or other stone you've empowered with you throughout the seven days and beyond as you see fit.

Whenever you encounter negative self-talk or thoughts about yourself during the week, write them down in as much detail as possible. Don't censor yourself; write freely with every fiber of your being. After the week has come to a close, delve deeper and work to find the root cause of these beliefs. You can share what you wrote with your therapist if you wish, and you can ask them to walk with you through deeper shadow work.

Close the spell after the seventh night by disassembling the altar and safely burning the paper containing negative self-talk. If any of the candle is left, meditate further with your shadow until it has burned down to your preference.

Inspiration Despite Hopelessness

Hopelessness can be dangerous; it implies that a person believes the future holds nothing worthwhile. If you experience hopelessness as a result of depression—especially if it's coupled with suicidal ideation—please seek professional help immediately.

I can say from experience that I've been there and, in the deepest trenches of hopelessness, life is worth continuing because hope *will* come back around when it's least expected. Don't forget the fact that you are a seeker of wisdom and that you have more capability than most to listen to the universe, observe synchronicities, and forge your own unique path. But how the hell do we define hopefulness in this disparaging world? In the brilliant words of musical artist Nick Cave, "Hope is optimism with a broken heart."[6]

This spell can be used in conjunction with professional assistance; we need to be our own best friends and advocates when faced with hard and necessary shadow work. Life has a strange way of lifting us back up and helping improve our trajectory; we must trust in the process and do whatever we can to ensure it.

Purchase a box or packet of your favorite oatmeal along with a small quantity of genuine maple syrup. The maple tree is said to help relieve depression, and oats are grounding, healthy, and yummy. Cook your oatmeal and bring it with you into a sacred space.

---

6. Nick Cave, *Faith, Hope & Carnage* (Picador Paper/Pan Macmillan, 2023), 271.

Next, make a poultice with the herb eyebright, best achieved by mixing powdered eyebright with a small amount of water. Eyebright is said to invoke hope *and* banish hopelessness. Sounds good to me!

Take off all your clothing (to be skyclad is sacred) and smear this poultice all over your brow. Smear it on other areas of the body as you see fit. Wash your hands and, after pouring the maple syrup into the oatmeal, cup your hands around the warm bowl and declare:

Rich sacred oats and sweet maple sap,
Comfort my heart and bring hope back!

Eat in silence and conclude the spell by showering off. Use either a salt scrub or a handful of salt to scrub your body with, which will help cast off stagnant, listless energy. Approach the day with the knowledge that you're consciously choosing to embrace a more uplifting experience of reality one day at a time.

Easing the Pain of Loneliness

The feeling of loneliness is utterly isolating. Those feelings are deeply personal yet are also fascinating to contemplate more objectively. The experience of being alone doesn't necessarily imply loneliness, just as one can feel lonely even when surrounded by others.

Getting to the root of loneliness takes time, patience, painfully honest reflection, and oftentimes assistance from others. In addition to real-world action for healing as well as perhaps finding genuinely like-minded individuals, this spell can amplify your intention and aid in the process.

The herb cinquefoil is called five-finger grass in Hoodoo traditions due to the leaves and petals appearing in formations of five segments. Each point is said to represent a different quality: love, money, health, power, and wisdom. Some historical mentions of the plant replace health with luck, but either way they're all fabulously desirable qualities. Cinquefoil is also said to help end loneliness.

Legendary author and the founder of the Reclaiming Witchcraft tradition Starhawk cites the energies of the plants aloe and nettles alongside any type of thorns to aid in remediating loneliness.[7]

On your altar, place a fresh apple atop a bed of cinquefoil. For added potency, you could also add cloves, rose quartz, or pink roses in some manner—all are said to promote friendships and new, compassionate connections.

Draw a pentagram on your bare chest to symbolize a link between the five-fingered cinquefoil and the starlike formation of the seeds inside the apple. You may draw this five-pointed star with sacred ink, a marker, or whatever feels correct.

With your hands cupped around the apple and herbs, state the following five times:

With courage, strength, and loneliness no more,
For new social connections I open a door.
I attract like-minded folks, I'm surrounded by love,
Within and without, below and above.

Conclude by cutting the apple in half, from top to bottom, so that the starlike formation of the seeds can be seen. Eat half of the apple in meditation as you focus on new friendships, relationships, and connections. Smile and visualize this occurring with ease.

---

7. Starhawk, *The Spiral Dance: A Rebirth of the Ancient Religion of the Great Goddess* (Harper, 1989), 178.

Sprinkle half the cinquefoil at your front door and offer the other portion along with the other half of the apple somewhere in the wilderness.

Combating Creative Blockages

Every creative and artistic person experiences blockages from time to time. These always prove to pass, but the interim can be altogether frustrating.

If you've been feeling uninspired, try sparking that flame again by doing a spell with sparklers. Sparklers are sold around New Year's (and Independence Day in the US) and are often available for purchase year-round in Chinatowns worldwide.

On a fresh piece of paper, draw the symbol displayed here, which is something I've created to represent breaking through blockages. This symbol is inspired in part by the product label used for the Lucky Mojo Curio Company's "Block Buster" bath salts, sachet powder, oil, and incense. One of my favorite authentic Hoodoo companies in the world, Lucky Mojo was founded by Catherine Yronwode, whose incredible book, *Hoodoo Herb & Root Magic: A Materia Magica of African-American Conjure,* was one of the many indispensable resources I consulted in this book's formation.

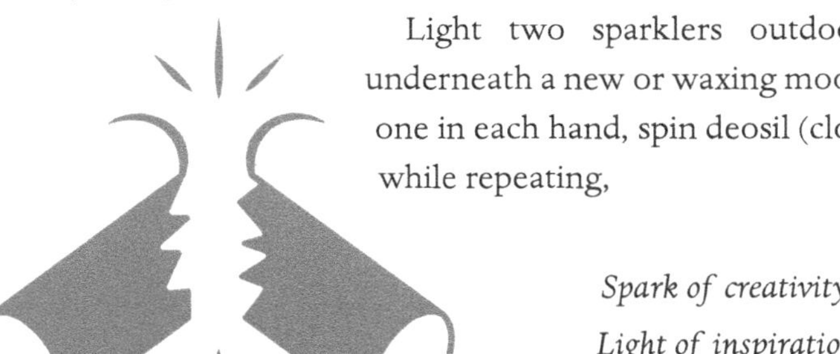

Light two sparklers outdoors and underneath a new or waxing moon. With one in each hand, spin deosil (clockwise) while repeating,

Spark of creativity!
Light of inspiration!
Come unto me, come unto me!

Repeat this three times and then burn the paper with the symbol. For added potency, consider wearing or carrying agate, sunstone, or jasper, all of which are said to inspire action. Also note that both rowan (mountain ash) and white sesame seeds are also used to inspire creativity, should you wish to incorporate either in your spell. If you are unable to procure sparklers at this time, simply substitute sticks of incense.

Countering Confusion & Overwhelm

Try this spell if you've been feeling confused, disoriented, mentally overwhelmed, or otherwise off-kilter. Can't seem to focus or think straight? This spell can be of assistance.

First, choose some stones and herbs. One mineral used to cast off confusion is the rose-colored gemstone rhodonite. Hematite is second-to-none for grounding. The flaky blue mineral kyanite is formed through intense pressure and heat, making it perfect for enduring the experience of overwhelming pressure. Peridot can be used to balance emotions and the mind, as can the herbs agrimony, cedar, and sage. Place a combination of any of these in a drawstring sachet bag or handmade pouch and wear it as a necklace specifically for this spell.

Put on relaxing music and meditate in peace for a while. When you feel ready, brush a fallen feather or leaf all over your body to help whisk away confusion and disorientation. Do this most especially around your head while you focus on intentional breathing. With every exhale, visualize the overwhelming energy being swept away.

When you feel settled, take deep breaths and anoint your head, neck, and brow with rosemary or lavender essential oil. I suggest the essential oil be diluted in a 10:1 ratio with a carrier oil such as jojoba, almond, or mineral oil (that is, one drop essential oil for every ten drops of carrier oil). Deeply inhale the herb's balancing essence, and conclude by giving thanks to your guides, guardians, and ancestors. Throw the feather or leaf outside.

Repeat this working when necessary. Set aside the herbal sachet so you can wear it when performing the spell again. You may also wear or carry the sachet privately when that sense of overwhelm returns.

Releasing Anger

Anger is considered a secondary emotion, that is, a reaction to deeper feelings of loss, sadness, betrayal, insecurity, physical pain, and so on. Anger, pessimism, and abrasiveness can be instinctive self-protection responses. There are many occasions when feelings of upset are absolutely justifiable. However, if felt too often or as a response to small inconveniences or disagreements, anger management should absolutely be sought by way of professional mental health assistance. Anger management teachings have proven beneficial for countless individuals. And for small bouts of anger and frustration, this spell can be of assistance.

In a secluded place outdoors, place an item on the ground that represents your anger. This could be a discarded hornet's nest, a handful of hot peppers, a drawing of an angry face, and so on.

Feel the anger rising within you. Allow the upset feelings boil and churn. When you're ready, stamp on, smash, pound, and spit on the object, conducting those angry feelings outside of your body. Once satisfied, sprinkle wormwood, dandelion, and/or passionflower on the object and around your body. Inhale the fresh air and let your heart rate calm down. Sense the comfort of the elements and bring to mind everything you're grateful for in life one thing at a time. Allow yourself to smile. Conclude by taking a bow and go about your day in peace.

If your item or items of focus are biodegradable, leave them in nature after the spell; otherwise, throw them in a public trashcan. For continued potency, wear a piece of fluorite any time anger rises to the surface, a stone believed to help provide relief.

Encouraging Emotional Regulation

Shadow workers are often highly sensitive, psychic, or empathic. We experience life's ups, downs, and all-arounds, and it's our job to keep these things in check. We must place our health first, physically, mentally, and emotionally. If the highs and lows are unbearably extreme, please seek mental health assistance immediately. For temporary experiences of emotional fluctuation, however, consider this spell as something helpful in your emotional journey.

The most powerful stones for helping balance emotions and the mind are kunzite, malachite, peridot, and moss agate. Wear a necklace or carry one of these stones both during this spell and whenever you're feeling noticeable emotional fluctuations.

At dusk, draw the symbol for Libra (displayed here) on one side of a piece of a paper and, on the opposite, write down all the conflicting thoughts, feelings, and emotions that are causing a temporary imbalance. Write anything and everything you feel, even if it seems awkward.

Read aloud what you've written, followed by stating,

My inner pendulum's been swinging 'round,
I must return to solid ground.
These things released and balance found,
I am now focused and grounded down.

Burn the paper outside in an abalone shell if you have one on hand. You may also wish to make a tea containing jasmine, lavender, sage, and/or anise, as these specifically assist with emotional regulation, as does the gemstone serpentine.

Finally, you could integrate dark or light molasses in the spell (blackstrap molasses is more bitter) by eating spoonfuls of your favorite variety throughout the ritual or eating a molasses cookie afterward with your tea. Molasses is known to encourage emotional regulation, and its consumption can serve to directly invoke this magickal quality.

Endurance During Hardship

Even during life's most difficult times, we have the opportunity to somehow hold out hope and carry on. In the face of crisis and stress, trusted family, friends, and emotional support professionals are essential. Difficult experiences need not become long-lasting traumas. This spell can assist during trying times.

First, choose an herb to work with based on its alleged magickal qualities: catnip promotes happiness, hawthorn lifts depression, eyebright transforms hopelessness into hope, borage cultivates happiness in the midst of challenge, rosemary invites optimism, lavender calms the senses, and cypress eases a mind in crisis.

With your herb or herbs of choice in a bowl before you, place the Chariot card of your favorite tarot deck upright in the middle. Sit and gaze at the imagery as you take in every detail. Among other things, the Chariot is a card of patience, the slow and steady climb to greater experiences and brighter times. Above all, it is a card of hope.

Take two pieces of hematite and hold one piece to each temple, just above your ears. Imagine the link between the two stones calming your thoughts. Feel your mind becoming grounded and balanced. Speak your wishes aloud to the card, asking its comforting energy of patience and perseverance to ease your mind and your path. Speak your wishes, hopes, and dreams aloud, and conclude by placing the pieces of hematite on either side of the card.

The next day, sprinkle the herb or herbs around your property and return the card to the middle of your deck. Because the Chariot is ruled by the zodiac sign Cancer, it's most powerful to perform this working when the Sun or Moon are in that sign, although this is by no means a requirement.

Recovering Quickly from Stress

If you're feeling suddenly stressed and overwhelmed but don't have time to slowly sit and process these feelings, try this brief act of magick to snap out of it.

Go to a private space and hyperventilate for a few seconds, quickly inhaling and exhaling: This represents your stress. Then, exhale slowly and deeply. At the next inhale, ring a loud bell all around your body. Ring the bell slower and softer while your breathing returns to normal. Repeat the word "present" as many times as feels natural.

Finally cease the ringing of the bell and take very deep breaths in through the nose and out the mouth. Feel your mind and energy now cleansed by way of sound. Place your hands in the *anjali* (prayer) mudra, bow, and smile. You've got this.

Banishing Bad Habits

Bad habits are common and can include anything from procrastination, negative thinking, neglecting personal needs, biting fingernails, playing with your hair, and on and on. Habits differ from addictions; please see the spell after this if you're suffering from addictive tendencies. Still, the two can go hand in hand, so both this spell and the following can be useful.

Mash or blend up a mixture of three common edible nightshades (plants from the family Solanaceae): a potato, a tomato, and an eggplant. Once pulverized or mashed and mixed, take a large jar that can hold the mixture and place a scoop in the bottom.

Cut thirteen pieces of white fabric or paper. On each, write the bad habit or list a variety of them. You can also choose to perform this with a coven or with family members who would like to participate.

Layer the fabric or paper one by one in the jar with the nightshade plant mixture between each strip. Finish by dumping the remainder of the mixture atop the final strip. As you layer each of the thirteen strips, declare the following with each:

Bad habits, bad tendencies, bad thoughts: begone!

Seal the jar and allow it to sit for thirteen days, ideally from a full moon to a new moon, and either throw it in the trash or empty the contents into a makeshift earth-dug grave.

Helping Break Addiction

Shadow workers are prone to heavy emotional and psychological experiences. As a result, escapism in various forms sometimes follows, including dependencies on certain substances, trains of thought, and manners of behavior. However, in its many forms, the shadow must be seen through. We can retrain our brains by creating healthy behavioral patterns and modes of thinking one day at a time.

Addictive behavior can take many forms: alcohol, drugs of any type, sex, porn, television, video games, social media scrolling, gambling, shopping, exercise, food, work, hoarding, being around certain people, and anything that causes a surge of dopamine to release in the body. There exist physical addictions, behavioral addictions, and impulse control disorders; these three types often overlap and may warrant further researching.

Dependencies are nothing to mess around with or take lightly, and they often require full abstinence or even rehabilitation on the road to recovery. Addictions are *not* habits—they are physiological and/or psychological dependencies and behaviors fundamentally rooted in discomfort with oneself and reality. In addition to pursuing professional treatment, this spell can help.

Think about the suffering you and others have endured as a result of the addiction. As you do so, burn a small amount of catnip or frankincense while holding amethyst in your left hand and obsidian in your right. Feel the amethyst's comforting energy entering your body; this stone is known to help break addictive tendencies. Strongly grip the obsidian while envisioning the addiction becoming absorbed by the stone. Say words of power while you do this, telling the addiction that it's no longer welcome in your life. Take as long as you need. Focus and feel the stone absorbing this hindrance.

When you feel a sense of relief, go outside and throw the obsidian far and away from your property. Cup the amethyst with both hands, allowing its healing energy to enter your body, mind, and spirit. Amethyst is also associated with balance, sobriety, and all-around healing. Keep this stone close to you regularly and throughout your commendable, wise, and courageous work in overcoming addiction. Congratulate yourself for choosing health and for choosing life. Whatever the road ahead looks like, you're taking one of many steps in the right direction.

When crafting additional spells and workings associated with breaking addiction, such as bath and shower sachets, the following herbs are distinctly known for assisting the process: catnip, frankincense, eucalyptus, hyssop, lavender, sage, High John the Conqueror root, lemongrass, ivy, black pepper, mullein, and (most especially) wormwood. Additional suggestions can be found in this book's section on correspondences.

Taming the Inner Critic

That critical voice inside all of us can convince us that the most awful things about ourselves, others, and life are true. Although that voice is there to protect us, it proves dangerous when out of hand. We need to catch the internal criticism when it arises, bring it into question to determine whether it's truly helpful in the moment.

Purchase a pack of small index cards and write critical word after word, or sentence after sentence, on each individual piece of paper. These may say "I am too (this)," "I'm not enough (this)," "Life is horrible," and so on. After you feel a sense of completion in writing these, take one piece of paper at a time and forcefully rip it in two.

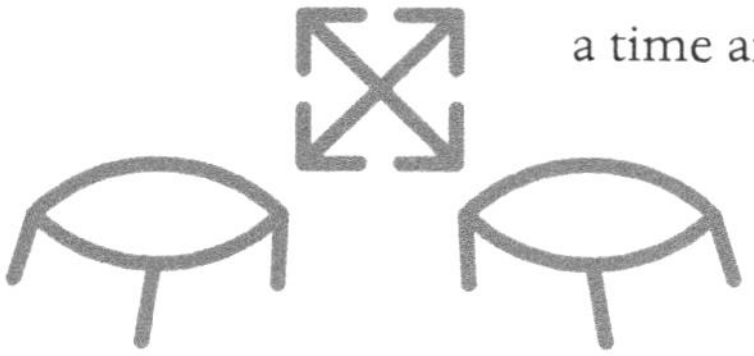

Throw the ripped pieces into a small bag upon which you've drawn the symbol shown here on either side. Spit on top of each piece as you do so, sending it away. Say the word "begone" with each rip and spit. Finalize the spell by sprinkling a handful of salt along with banishing herbs into the bag. Suggestions for these include nettles, wormwood, mugwort, rue, angelica, mullein, and cloves. See the correspondences section under "Banishing & Releasing" for additional suggestions.

Shake up the bag and bring it to your local post office to help send it off, so to speak by dumping out the bag in the post office's public trashcan. Throw away the paper bag as well. Seal the spell by speaking your own words of power or a simple "So mote it be!"

Stop Hating Yourself, Dammit!

We can convince ourselves of the most horrible things, and that's gotta stop. When that voice inside gets unruly and we start believing ourselves to be less than, we need to get our thoughts in check. Regret and depression can ensue if we're consumed by self-loathing. Whether in the form of shame, guilt, or embarrassment, self-deprecation is *not* our friend. Instead, we need to become our own best friends.

In her lovely book *Shadow Magic: Unlocking the Whole Witch Within*, Nikki Van De Car writes:

> When we look inward, we often have a very difficult time finding things to love—even though that is precisely where true self-love exists. This is just part of the reality of being human in this day and age; self-love is hard to find. This has absolutely nothing to do with you or your own *worthiness*—it's simply that we are so often caught up in daily challenges and expectations

> that we let the best parts of ourselves become buried. The light can be as hidden as the shadow.[8]

Self-love yourself, baby. Create an herbal blend consisting of any of the following: catnip, flax, ginseng, life everlasting, thyme, rose, rosemary, sunflower, and vervain. These are renowned for increasing self-love, self-appreciation, and self-confidence.

With these herbs held before you in sacred space, visualize them coming to life and glowing with a solar light of strength, fortitude, and gratitude for your gift of consciousness. Think about how far you've come in life and visualize how far you'll go. Loving and respecting yourself is an act of bravery, recognition, and wisdom. It's only upward from here.

Enchant the herbs both with this visualization and by saying the following nine times:

Love from within and love from without,
I invoke joy in life's journey throughout.

Use these herbs in any manner your intuition deems fit and be sure to enchant them further by soaking under direct sunlight. Burn them as incense, carry them on your person, make 'em into tea, craft a magickal bath blend, and so on. The herbal mixture is your friend just as you deserve to be your own best friend and advocate in life.

---

8. Nikki Van De Car, *Shadow Magic: Unlocking the Whole Witch Within* (Running Press/Hachette Book Group, 2023), 97.

Balancing Shadow & Light

We all have a battle of darkness and light within us. While it would be silly to equate dark and light with good and bad, our human language is limited. This spell requires the awareness of uplifting versus destructive thoughts within us. If these thoughts are proving toilsome, invoke the energy of oak to help balance the internal struggle.

Mindfully harvest or acquire either two oak tree branches, two oak leaves, or two acorns. Bind these together in an X formation using red string or thread.

Holding the charm before you, state:

Powerful oak, great grounding tree,
Balance my dark and light, so mote it be.

Hang this indoors where you will see it often and be reminded of oak's mighty balancing power. May it also remind you of your own ability to balance conflicting thoughts and emotions that arise.

Inspiration Through Struggle

It's natural for every mystic to go through periods of doubting the sacred nature of life. This is especially true if things have not been working in our favor and feelings of distress have taken over. We might know rationally that there is always hope, but our emotions can at times convince us otherwise.

This is a simple spell for enchanting an item to make the struggle let up a little bit.

One way to increase optimism and gain inspiration in life is to empower a necklace of citrine, whether as a wrapped stone or a necklace made of citrine chips.

On a bright, sunny day, anoint your necklace with citrus oil or the juice of orange, lemon, or lime. Present the necklace to the sun while stating:

Citrine empowered with hope and with life,
this radiant light shall overcome all strife!

Wear the necklace during any time of sadness, pessimism, sluggishness, or overthinking.

CHAPTER 3

Spells Concerning the Future

When it comes to internal shadow work concerning the future, we overwhelming discover the theme of fear. Fear is very much normal and natural, and is part of every species' evolutionary process (don't go messing with mama bear, for example!). Left unregulated, however, fear can become a destructive force that impedes everyday functioning.

The spells in this chapter focus greatly on anxiety and negative thinking, namely in regard to future scenarios. The truth is that we don't know where life will take us, so it's important to prepare ourselves for whatever life has in store.

You will also find spells that focus on preparation in a different manner. These include preparing for body modification, preparing to receive helpful services from others, and even preparing for birthdays. The reason is that for many people, shadows of insecurity, shame, and anxiety surround these types of occasions.

This chapter's spells and workings are primarily aimed at alchemizing negative thinking into something lighter; something more manageable and positive. Simply put, the invocation of confidence is monumental in the process of resolving fear. Confidence in ourselves and in our life's work, both magickal and otherwise, allows us to more bravely face and forge the road ahead.

Breaking Through Anxiety

Anxiety is often considered fear about future scenarios, and it is a subject much too deep to explore in these pages. Many people drawn to shadow work have anxiety episodes or disorders, and they find solace in working with unknown and mysterious forces. Perhaps this provides a sense of security by way of directive action.

Try this spell as one component of working with anxiety. Additionally, please consider counseling, cognitive-behavioral therapy, and other forms of professional assistance. We all deserve to feel safe in our lives, and this spell can assist when anxiety becomes too overwhelming.

Buy a fresh coconut and enter a sacred space outdoors beneath a full moon (if possible). Perform calming breathwork while grasping the coconut, envisioning your anxiety and fears entering the object. Shake it up, invigorating the coconut with fear. Once finished, throw it to the ground and, before smashing it with hammer, declare:

Fears and anxieties now begone!
I claim my power; I'm safe and strong!

Leave the smashed coconut in nature and turn around without looking back.

For extra force, integrate the Hoodoo root devil's shoestring (goat's rue) in some manner, whose energy is believed to banish blockages such as anxiety while simultaneously invoking luck and protection.

Abating the Fear Cycle

Fears and anxieties are, evolutionarily, designed to protect us. When this manner of thinking overtakes a person to the point of interfering with everyday life, it's usually a sign of a mental health condition that deserves treatment. Perpetual fear stops our forward momentum, convincing us of awful things about ourselves, about others, and about the nature of life itself.

If fear has been intense lately, one way to help manage it is to get some sidewalk chalk and write down every fear you can bring to mind, ideally on a full or waning moon and even better if the moon is in Virgo or Gemini, as they are ruled by Mercury.

If you don't have a private sidewalk available, get a chalkboard to adapt the spell. When you've written down everything you can think of, cross everything off with a large chalk X, spit at what you've written, and, using your own words, command these thoughts to go away for good.

Sweep the chalk in a widdershins (counterclockwise) manner using a besom (broom), and once the words are barely legible, sprinkle the dried herbs yarrow and nettles atop, as well as a handful of salt. Note that you should only use a small portion of salt outdoors because it can be damaging to plants and ecosystems.

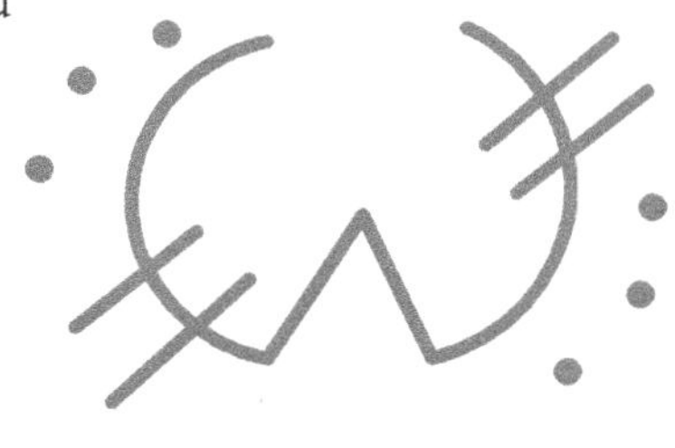

The next day, spray it down with yarrow tea (ideally) or fresh water, washing away each overwhelming thought.

Finalize the spell by chalking the symbol on the previous page, which is designed to work against fear, on the top of your now-cleansed magickal workspace.

Additionally consider creating a sachet bag of yarrow, nettles, and either carnelian or citrine, all said to help break fearful cycles and increase confidence in facing life's ups and downs. Herbal alternatives (or additions) to yarrow and nettles can be found in the correspondences section under "Fear, to ease " as well as additional suggestions for working with fear.

Averting Catastrophic Thinking

Catastrophizing is a cognitive process of expecting or assuming the worst possible outcome in any given situation and is generally the result of negative conditioning from past experiences. No one deserves to feel as though life will always be a letdown or that horrible things will take the place of anything good. Not only is this mindset unrealistic, it's unfair to you—it minimizes the potential you have for making changes or exercising your free will. Please seek professional therapeutic assistance if mental catastrophizing is an ongoing issue that interferes with your everyday functioning and happiness in life.

To help avert catastrophic thinking and its accompanying paranoia, try freezing a string of hot peppers. Get a variety of fresh, spicy peppers from a local market or farmer, and string them together by puncturing or tying them into a bundle (ideally with red string). Submerge the string of peppers underwater in an airtight bag. As you stick the bundle in the back of the freezer, say:

Horrific thinking, paranoid brain,
I expect the worst again and again.
Now these thoughts I bound and gag,
Never to return again. So mote it be.

Once the ongoing paranoid, catastrophic thinking lets up, simply throw the spell in the trash.

Releasing Self-Obsession

One side effect of insecurity is self-obsession, which can take form as a fixation about our identity, whether socially or physically, or an unrealistic idea of perfectionism. At the end of the day, perpetual self-criticism creates obsession and ultimately lowers our self-image. If you've been beating yourself up and getting down on yourself in a prominent, perpetual way, try this spell. Although there is always room for improvement, unhealthy obsessions with our image and character are very much a manifestation of anxiety.

Strip fully skyclad (nude) and stand before a mirror, ideally full-length. Take deep breaths and allow yourself to view your body as a nonjudgmental outsider. Invoke the energy of curiosity, thinking to yourself, "What a fascinating human frame," and "I wonder how this biomechanical creature thinks and functions."

Shift this energy to appreciation, noticing your body's unique curves, angles, and unique features. Smile, whispering words such as "fascinating" and "beautiful," bringing a subtle smile to your face. Look in your eyes and do the same, entranced by the beauty of the face and depth of the eyes looking back at you. Compliment your beautiful brain and body.

Finally, shift to a mentality of gratitude. Speak these words of thanks:

Spirits divine, through space and through time,
Here I exist in this brain, this body, this mind.
I offer gratitude and the deepest of thanks,
I am sacred, unique, and an expression of grace.

Finalize by showering or bathing, perhaps even sensually masturbating, and then by wearing sacred garments and jewelry, or another form of expressing self-appreciation. To seal the spell, think of some sort of volunteer work you can do to help others in need, whether human, animal, or environmental, as shifting your focus onto assisting others can instill in you a healthy sense of pride, confidence, and hope.

Gender & Sexuality Confidence

If you find yourself struggling with confidence in gender identity or sexual orientation, you're not alone. LGBTQ+ individuals find themselves in varying degrees of acceptance versus danger depending on the culture. If your mental or physical health are at risk, please contact appropriate authorities and/or urgent mental health assistance. We all deserve to live in safety, equanimity, and peace of mind, even in the face of our rights and freedoms being scrutinized and sabotaged.

It's good to keep in mind that queer folks of all varieties have long been held sacred and are still highly regarded in numerous cultures whose deepest roots haven't been entirely colonized. We have existed for as long as humankind, are very much part of the normal and natural order of evolutionary reality, and we're here to stay. Whoever you are and however you are, you are beautiful. This meditative spell is contained here in the future section of this chapter due to its ties with identity and anxiety.

In addition to the preceding spell, consider regularly increasing self-love and confidence by focusing specifically on the *svadhisthana* (sacral) chakra. The sacral chakra is connected to issues of sexuality, self-image, and confidence.

To begin, light an orange candle. Then brew a tea consisting of any of these herbs, all associated with self-confidence in both gender and sexuality: lavender, catnip, angelica, clover, and blue lotus. Additionally, you could cut up a fresh orange and eat some of the fruit before and after meditating. Otherwise, sip half of the tea before meditating and the other half afterward. Be sure to offer a bit of the tea and/or slice of orange outdoors after you're done.

In a safe, sacred space, sit either cross-legged or in a chair with hands resting in your lap. Cradle the right hand atop the left and allow your thumbs to barely touch. This particular hand posture, called the *dhyana mudra*, can also be researched online; it is portrayed in a great deal of Hindu and Buddhist iconography.

You may wish to rest a gemstone in your hands that is associated with this chakra—the most renowned are carnelian, sunstone, and orange calcite. Because this working is specifically for those struggling with gender and/or sexuality, also consider amethyst due to its associations with queer magick (alternatives are rose quartz and angelite). For additional ideas, feel free to check out both the listings "Confidence" and "LGBTQ+ Magick" in the correspondences section.

Now that you're all set up with the tea and fruit as well as the candle or stone(s), take deep breaths, close your eyes, and calm your mind. Become comfortable in body and mind, and bring your focus to the sacral chakra. See it swirling in a gorgeous, vibrant, comforting, deep orange color. Visualize this color growing strong and serene, blasting off shadowy blockages that may appear as dark shades in your mind's eye. You're likely to feel a sensation of heat beneath the navel.

As you do so, simply repeat the ancient *bija mantra* ("seed" sound) for this chakra, *vam* (pronounced "vahhm"). Repeat this quietly, loudly, silently, or however you see fit. Feel each syllable entering this chakra, providing comfort and balance. Know that you are sacred, brave, and unique.

Come back to your body and give thanks to the Powers That Be. Repeat this working as often as you see fit, and consider researching and integrating *full* chakra alignment practices to increase wellness of body, mind, and spirit.

Preparing for Body Modification

If you're planning on getting a tattoo, a piercing, an elective surgical procedure, a cosmetic surgery, or another type of body modification, take a little time beforehand to prep the body and mind.

Get comfortable and ask for your guides and guardians to be present. In your own words, verbally ask for their protection in the procedure, and extend gratitude for their help. Explain to them your intention in receiving alteration of the body, including any medical or metaphysical associations you intend with the procedure, such as wherever you're receiving a piercing, the design of the tattoo's ink, or the area of the body undergoing treatment. Declare these things aloud to connect with your spoken spell.

Gently focus on the area that will become modified either by touching the area or seeing it in your mind's eye. See it glowing in pure, pristine, white light.

Talk to that area directly by saying the following ten times:

Soon you will be altered; body and spirit hear me now,
My intentions have been stated, those truths I do vow,
This (tattoo/piercing/procedure) is my crafted spell,
Changes will occur and all will be well.

Preparing to Receive a Service

The process of healing services involve shadow work to some extent, no matter the modality or method. If you're feeling anxious about receiving help or healing from another person, it's wise to prepare the mind. The service you're about to receive could be a medical or therapeutic appointment, a tarot or spiritual reading, a massage, energy healing session, or anything else that requires putting yourself out there. We are all here to help each other in life, and it can be both enjoyable and beneficial to open oneself to others' assistance.

Humility and honesty are necessary components of receiving service. Feelings of vulnerability and worthiness can arise for many people who are receiving a service or assistance from someone else. Simply opening up can be shadowy work for those who have long felt unworthy or who are understandably skeptical of fellow humans in general.

"Taking one's measure" is practice in the initiation rites of British Traditional Wicca that helps positively bind a person to their coven. To make use of this method in a personal manner, gather a pair of scissors alongside string, thread, or twine. Measure from the tip of each middle finger to get your full wingspan, and make a cut. Snip another piece from head to toe, and a third in the measure of your waist.

The reason for taking your measure in the context of a spell for receiving a service is because the measure represents you as you are, in this body and at this time. Whatever relationship you have with body image, the cord's measure doesn't lie. This signifies the honest presentation of yourself to a healer or helper; they can more acutely perform services by objectively assessing who you are at present.

Bundle up these pieces in a drawstring sachet or bag, and add herbs, stones, or written words of power that represent confidence (see correspondences beginning on page 248). You can carry this bag on person when receiving services or assistance. Finish the spell by holding the bag at your heart and declaring the following three times:

This bag of measure is anointed with strength,
Containing my height, my width, and my length.
Open mind and open heart, I hereby vanquish all doubt;
I welcome sacred services within and throughout.

Preparing for a Birthday

While many consider them a cause for celebration, birthdays can also be an awkward time for many folks. The occasions carry memories of birthdays past and can bring to mind ideas of self-assessment or even judgment. For those working with issues of confidence, birthdays can be a time of sadness and reflection. If you feel as though you haven't met personal expectations at whatever age you are turning, try going easy on yourself and remember that there's plenty of time ahead.

To prepare your mind against potential self-deprecation, perform this spell shortly before your birthday, ideally once daily beginning six days before the day. Six is a number of confidence and is associated with the sun; this is appropriate because birthdays are Solar returns: the day when the sun returns to the same place it was in conjunction to Earth when you were born.

Acquire traditional van van oil, which is an all-purpose recipe of amplification. I consider it similarly to quartz crystal in that it can be used to boost the intention of any spell or prayer. In Hoodoo and related magickal systems, van van primarily contains lemongrass, although some commercial varieties simply use a blend lemon oil and wood alcohol.[9] The term *van van* is likely an old mispronunciation of the herb "vervain," hinting that the traditional recipe likely contained some amount of this plant. Additionally, verbena is sometimes called vervain, although the two are actually different plants. Verbena is much easier to make into essential oil, so traditional van van blends will often contain some amount of this as well. Note that verbena and lemon verbena are not the same plants but both are part of the Verbenaceae family.

If you can't find van van oil, simply make a tea containing lemongrass, blue vervain, and/or verbena. Anoint your chest, wrists, and neck with the essential oil or tea, and either wear or carry a stone associated with the sun and with confidence; examples of these include citrine, carnelian, and sunstone.

Standing beneath the sun, envision solar energy entering your body and aura. Bow deeply in gratitude for the life-giving force of sunlight and repeat the following six times:

9. John Michael Greer, *The New Encyclopedia of the Occult* (Llewellyn Publications, 2003), 500.

Van van vibration, van van validation,
My birthday gives rise to all these sensations.
Conquering sun, I learned from this year,
I welcome you back; outshine doubt and fear.
Solar return, enhance my inner light,
That I may shine by day and by night!

Embracing a Saturn Return

Similarly to how a Solar Return occurs once a year, one's "Saturn birthday" occurs approximately every twenty-nine years. The exact time for a person's Saturn returns can be calculated by a professional astrologer or by some programs on the internet. These can be celebrated as rare and *very* special occasions. Sometimes Saturn will even perform a retrograde during one's Return, giving a "triple whammy" while it does its return, appears to go backwards from Earth's perspective, and once again "returns" in the chart. This spell can be performed on one or each of these occasions.

Saturnal, Saturnian, or Saturnine energy encompasses the big picture: life, death, karma, experiential wisdom, rebirth, self-discipline, harsh life lessons, and the process of aging. Saturn aligns with the Great Goddess (divine feminine) in esoteric Qabalah under the third sefira, Binah. Perform this spell on or around the time of one of your life's Saturn returns.

After researching the qualities of Saturn, take the four threes—the Three of Wands, Cups, Swords, and Pentacles respectively—from a deck of tarot cards and place them before you. Light a black candle and burn myrrh incense while meditating on each card's qualities and spiritual meaning.

When you're ready, declare the following thrice:

Binah, Great Mother, Ama and Aima,
Behold my Return of Saturn!
I have grown, lived, loved, and look ahead.
Blessings to Saturn, mighty force of life.
I honor the past and walk forward in wisdom!

Return the four tarot cards in random places to your deck and take a relaxing bath or shower while contemplating your long-term goals. Most importantly, recognize how far you've come—there's a long way to go, and it truly is a blessing through thick and thin!

Section II

Interpersonal Shadow Spells

Shadow Reflection: Magickal Paradox

Successful results are best yielded with an ethical approach to the magickal arts; we should always honor our intuitive moral compass!

Something to be aware of when casting magick of any kind is the potential for *paradox*. Similarly to a crash following a high, when energies and intentions are strong, a paradoxical effect may follow. Challenges, tests, and seemingly opposing energies to what a person has cast can manifest for a couple days or longer.

Cast a spell for money and the next week get overcharged for something? A spell for happiness, and the next day you feel like crap? A cord-cutting and then the person comes at you with a vengeance? That's paradox energy!

If these sorts of things happen to you, give it some time. Don't nullify any of this post-spell chaos or it can nullify the original magick that's actually doing its thing! Just give it a little time to settle. Although the occasional rebound feels discouraging in the moment, that backswing of the pendulum is a sign that your magick is indeed weaving into reality.

Shadow Reflection: Taglocks & Ousia

The terms "taglock" and "personal concerns/personal effects" are used in Hoodoo, Rootwork, Conjure, and related systems. They are similar to the Greek concept of *θεία ουσία* (*theia ousia*; sometimes shortened to *ousia*) meaning divine essence, substance, or beingness. It is the essence of a person.[10]

This link is of particular importance in magick concerning oneself and another. In a pinch, a virtual photo, a sketch, or the person's written name can suffice, as can a personal belonging or even a footprint. The strongest magickal taglock, however, is anything that contains DNA.

When it comes to personal shadow magick, you could use a sterile lancet to draw a few drops of your own blood, but hair and fingernails can also work. Anyone with a history of self-harm should shy away from drawing blood for magickal work; professional tattoos and piercings are highly recommended alternate forms of catharsis!

> Professions and practices focused on healing, on any level, are very much related to shadow work. To invite healing is to acknowledge that which is imbalanced.

10. *Wikipedia*, s.v. "ousia," accessed April 23, 2025, https://en.wikipedia.org/wiki/ousia.

CHAPTER 4

Protection & Shielding

When it comes to interpersonal shadow work; that is, how we interact with shadowy energy that originates from other people, protection is of utmost importance. In the same way that we would protect our physical bodies from harm, that same impetus extends to the metaphysical world.

In this chapter you'll find both old and new methods of energetic protection and shielding. It's not always necessary to know the source of harmful shadowy energy that you've picked up. In many cases, as we will explore, this energetic gathering is unintentional and unconscious.

Protection magick can be beneficial if you feel that harmful vibes have been sent in your direction. It can also be helpful preemptively, so this chapter includes spells and charms focused on boundaries, shields, and protective wards. It is good practice to regularly craft and maintain several of these charms rather than taking a one-and-done approach.

If you feel the call to energetically guard yourself, odds are that your intuition is guiding you to do so. These spells and charms can certainly assist in this process!

Protection by Witch Bottle

What's often called a witch bottle is one of the oldest methods of protection to date. Renowned since ancient times, magickal bottles that protect a person against all forms of external negativity are a natural response to the challenges of being a member of a social species. Witch bottles and related spells don't necessarily have to protect against a single person in particular; they are equally effective against destructive energy that comes from outside sources.

The simplest way of constructing a witch bottle is to gather a variety of sharp objects and pokey components to place in tight-sealing a glass jar, ideally a mason jar. Sharp items are used to capture and slay external negativities, and can include things such as rusty nails, shards of glass or mirror, tacks, staples, screws, and thorns. Chips from black gemstones are recommended, namely obsidian, onyx, and black tourmaline. Herbal ingredients are optional, and may include cloves, asafoetida (hing), cat's claw, garlic, belladonna, agrimony, digitalis (foxglove), hawthorn, henbane, mandrake, hemlock, mullein, nettles, black pepper, hot peppers, tobacco, wormwood, datura (thorn apple/jimsonweed), and valerian.

Ideally on the day of a full moon or dark moon, fill the bottle with your morning urine. Your pee not only links the spell to you personally, but it also represents releasing, banishing, and removing toxic energies; in this case, the vibes you're not permitting to enter! Add a splash of vinegar; ideally Four Thieves vinegar if you have it on hand. Additional components may include cobwebs, snakeskin, an owl pellet, and fingernail clippings. If you're protecting a household with pets, collect a small amount of their feces or urine (such as from a cat litter box). If your jar is aimed at protecting anyone else living in the household, you could ask them to (at the very least and unless they're freaked out by the idea) spit in the jar—*before* you pee in it, that is!

Enchant the concoction in any way you deem fit and is aligned with your personal beliefs and practices. Hide or bury the bottle either somewhere outside your front door or in an indoor location that feels appropriate. Many so-called witch bottles in the ancient world were discovered by archaeologists under or around a person's hearth or fireplace. There is no need to cover it with a cloth, as this would shroud the magick, but it's certainly advisable to place it in a dark location where only you (and fellow casters, if relevant) know its location.

In some practices both modern and in the ancient world, the protective bottle is buried, never to be disturbed again in one's lifetime—or at least for the duration the property is occupied by whomever did the spellwork. Do what you feel is best. Personally, I like to replace my witch bottle every 366 days (a year and a day). I also make a new one if I move to a new location and make sure to toss old ones in the trash. Landfilling an old witch bottle ensures that the sharp objects and biomatter won't eventually unearth and harm someone. I also replace a witch bottle if I psychically sense the current one is energetically full or something else indicates that it has run its course, such as if the bottle inexplicably falls over in the middle of the night. I also like to superglue the lid shut once it's filled to avoid nasty leakage, and to burn a black candle on top of the jar to seal it both physically and metaphysically. As with all spells, customize and personalize the working to your own preferences and intuitive impressions.

A Traveling Witch Bottle (Guest Spell)

The following spell is written by my Witchy friend Catherine Lee Cunningham, who recently released her first book of magickal poetry and artwork (see the bibliography). I was pleased to stay with Catherine and her family during a book tour, and we've stayed in touch ever since. When she told me about this spell she had created, I simply couldn't resist including it here!

At a time when I was feeling hostility at work, coupled with the political and social climate in the country and world, I put together this nontraditional traveling witch bottle. Its primary purpose is for protection when leaving the house and venturing into society. I wanted something small and portable that I could take with me for this purpose and, when the bottle was present at home, it would naturally protect the house and family.

The ingredients are as follows: a small, portable bottle with a cap (cork stoppers are not ideal for travel), angelica root, belladonna or a related nightshade, dragon's blood resin, mandrake root (substitute American mayapple), essential oil of frankincense, a pinch of black salt (see page 171), a pinch of red brick dust (a common ingredient in Hoodoo), shielding oil or protection oil (optional premade blends), and three small nails. Top this off with a base oil; I prefer almond, but you may opt for mineral, jojoba, or something different. Add a drop of your own blood if you wish or a fingernail clipping.

As you add each ingredient to the bottle, charge it with your intent to be protected when you are on the go. Blow your breath into the bottle, infusing the spell with your personal essence. Tightly seal the bottle and shake it up. Leave it on your altar overnight to absorb the peaceful energy of your sacred space. If desired, the bottle can be charged by the light of the moon. Carry it with you in a bag or on person for protection both from free-floating negativity and from ill will directed toward you from others.

Protection by Nails & Citrus

A fun, striking charm for protection that originates in Italy makes use of a citrus fruit, normally a lemon. The fruit is traditionally stuck with nine nails and bound in red thread. Left to hang, aversive energy is said to enter the fruit instead of the caster.

Some folks prefer to use needles or pins instead of nails and additionally choose a numerologically significant number to poke into the fruit. The charm is then hung within the home, ideally in an area that receives a good amount of foot traffic. As it shrivels up and changes color, it indicates the fruit is actively absorbing bad vibes.

With each penetration of the citrus by nails or needles, state something appropriate, such as "negativity into *here*" or "all harmful energy is trapped *here*!"

Once the fruit has hardened and turned black, either remove the nails and needles (they can be cleansed and reused as you see fit) and bury the fruit somewhere off property, or simply toss the whole thing in the trash.

Protection by Cactus

Due to their pokey nature, cacti are renowned plants of protection near and far. Simply purchase a small potted cactus (or a number of them), and follow their easy care instructions. You may wish to enchant the plant by saying something like this:

Cactus plump and cactus sharp,
Protect my home, protect my heart.

I honor your life as you guard my own,
Your presence is strong here in this home.

Nobody has to know that your cactus is a magickal charm; houseplants are not out of the ordinary. Otherwise, if you're well out of the broom closet, feel free to incorporate it with other charms that clearly display it as an intentional ward.

Protection by Hagstone

Hagstones are rocks, large or small, into which the ocean has naturally worn a hole or a number of holes. They also go by the names witch stone, faery stone, holey stone, and mare-stone, to name a few. Legend has it that one can even get a glimpse of the faery realm by gazing through a naturally holed stone.

For our purposes of protection, you can either find one of these stones on a beach, at your local metaphysical supplier, or from an online retailer. Be sure to confirm that the stone was formed by nature rather than drilled by machine.

As the mighty sea has weathered its magick on the ancient stone, honor this powerful energy as you string it with a cord and say:

Pounding ocean, mother of life,
I honor this stone that protects me from strife.
Wherever it hangs, all evil must flee,
As I do will, so shall it be!

From my studies, it seems that string, thread, or twine colored red is the most common for suspending folk charms. I have also found black material quite effective for the purpose, though I tend to default to something all-natural such as cotton or jute twine depending on the spell.

You may choose to suspend the hagstone from the ceiling in your home, by your bed, or craft one into a special necklace pendant; the options are vast as the sea!

Protection by Talons

Across time and culture, the feet and talons of birds have been used as protective folk charms. There's no strict manner of crafting a charm of this sort. Whether a bound-up bundle of bird feet nailed above the front door or a simple lonesome talon added to a bundle of protective herbs, this sort of charmery is both creative and effective.

Naturally, put some thought and consideration into how you will acquire a foot or talon. Many online magickal suppliers and taxidermy shops sell these body parts for occult and artistic purposes. Or maybe you or a friend raise fowl for food. Whatever the case, *don't* kill an animal simply for one of its body parts; to do so is inevitably a curse. If obtained fresh and locally, even by bravely asking a farmer to save the feet from its next slaughtered bird, be sure to pack the foot in salt until it's properly dried. If purchased from a taxidermist or occult supplier, the foot or talon is likely ready for use.

Enchant the object in whatever manner feels proper to you. Spend time communicating with the oversoul of the animal whose foot or talon you're using, being sure to research their associations in a book like *Animal Speak* by Ted Andrews as well as online resources. Offer prayers for the specific animal's afterlife and extend heartfelt gratitude.

If you don't feel comfortable using animal bits, choose instead to make use of sharp thorns and twigs. Successful results are best yielded with an ethical approach to the magickal arts; we should always honor our intuitive moral compass.

Protection by Onion

Onions have long been renowned in multiple cultures for their ability to capture and counter harmful energy. A simple charm that you can incorporate alongside other protective measures is to cut two onions in half, wrap each half in string (red or black are ideal), and hang them up in the four corners of your home or room. This can be repeated in additional rooms, and you may even choose to align them elementally in the four cardinal directions.

Alternatively, the next time you grab an onion for cooking, do something similar with the inedible ends you cut off each side. Get creative and have fun engaging with onion's protective properties!

Trapping a Hex

A fun, spooky, Witchy charm to capture and contain external negative energy is a triangular trap made of twigs. Whether someone has been petty enough to curse you or you're simply feeling cautious about the effects of slander, a charm of this nature is sure to help guard against vibes that serve no constructive purpose.

The purpose of this folksy charm is to confuse the energy of intentional *and* unintentional curses, hexes, and otherwise harmful energies projected in your direction.

Determine the size of the trap or traps you wish to craft, and be sure to research the metaphysical properties of the tree or shrub whose wood you are utilizing. Mindfully secure and uniformly snip a number of twigs or small branches to bind together in four uniform sections. Fallen twigs are best for this purpose, as to not harm the tree … unless it's trimming season.

Use one row of twigs for the bottom, two for the sides, and one for the back, leaving a "door" in the front for negative energy to enter. In this fashion, there is no "roof," as the triangular sides create the structure. Considering this configuration, you may wish to trim the back portion of twigs into a triangular shape.

Attach the little house to a string or plan to tuck it somewhere hidden. This charm should be hung outdoors. Inside the trap, add bits of your hair and fingernail clippings, as this will guide the negative energy to the structure rather than your person. Add a tangled mess of black sewing thread, which confuses the energy, and finish by including cloves and thorns. Use your intuition to enchant the charm with the purpose of harmful external energies being directed to the trap. Don't be afraid to forcefully state this purpose, as you are pointedly casting away, misdirecting, and capturing harmful vibes.

After three moon cycles or when your intuition guides, remove the charm, throw it on the earth, add a good amount of the herb agrimony, and stomp on it with force. Spit at the item and sprinkle salt upon the remnants (ideally black salt; see page 171). Finish by throwing the item in a public trashcan to send it far and away. Repeat as necessary.

Psychic & Empathic Shielding

We are all a little bit psychic and a little bit empathic—or a lot! I was fortunate enough to spend years researching and writing books about empathy specifically, and I've come to realize that higher psychic or emotional sensitivity quite often require energetic shielding for increased health and wellbeing.

There is one gemstone that stands out from the rest when it comes to psychic and empathic protection: black tourmaline. Although other gemstones are protective in a variety of ways, I have found that black tourmaline takes center stage for this specific purpose. Please note that black tourmaline should not be worn or carried on a daily basis due to its potency in energetic shielding! Instead, the stone is best used on an as-needed basis, such as when preparing for highly public experiences, giving a presentation, or being around people of whose energies you're a bit cautious.

Simply acquire a necklace made of black tourmaline; a basic wire-wrapped stone or a chipped gemstone strand will do just fine. Also acquire two small, separate pieces of black tourmaline to carry in each pocket. You will sense which pieces call to you and can rely on intuition to guide you regarding when and how to wear or carry the pieces.

In a sacred space, enter a meditative state and call upon your spirit helpers. After running the stones through pure, fresh water, lovingly place them before you and speak this enchantment while visualizing them *and* you surrounded in crystalline light:

Mother Earth on whom I tread, I approach you with this plea,
Guard my mind and emotions when I am in need.
Just as darkness cloaks, comforts, and protects,
Such blessings come alive through these objects.
Holy tourmaline, shadow rampart and shield,
You are my sacred ally; from harm I am concealed!

Boundaries with Bones

Many sensitive people struggle to define their personal needs. Social boundaries consist of behaviors or statements (which needn't be rude) specifically focused on what you, yourself choose to engage with or disengage from. Boundaries communicate our needs and are an act of self-respect. Boundaries are your own terms and conditions. An example of a boundary is stating something like, "I won't continue this conversation if you continue to use insults." Note how this statement concerns your own personal needs rather than demanding the other party change their ways.

In addition to working on boundaries by way of spoken or written communication, a charm to help confidently establish boundaries is as follows. Procure a red flannel sachet bag (or stitch one up yourself). Find two small dried bones of any type (dried chicken bones work great), or substitute by using artificial bones, such as those used in Halloween decorations. Affix these bones in an X shape either on the front of the bag or bound together with black or red thread and placed inside.

In addition to salt of any type, the most potent herbs associated with establishing boundaries are yarrow, nettles, and dragon's blood resin. Place a combination of these inside your bag along with a small slip of paper containing a written prayer, sigil, or symbol that represents social boundaries. For extra protection, add a small hematite stone and a pinch of sand. You may also wish to see the correspondences section, namely "Boundaries, to establish."

Enchant the charm as you wish—you could bless it with the elements or direct sunlight. Sunlight specifically will help counteract the shadow of shyness, fear, social expectations, or whatever has been holding you back from accurately asserting boundaries and needs.

To seal the spell, speak the following into the completed bag five times:

Charm of red with bones inside,
Minerals and herbs, now come alive!
My boundaries are mine; all safe and aligned,
I now become confident, for I am divine.
Kept safe from harm, I establish my way,
My rules are my own, and within these I stay!

Once the bag is sealed or stitched up, you may choose to carry it in your pocket or handbag in social situations, or incorporate it in a greater ritualistic working. Get methodical; for example, if you have an office or work from home and are experiencing boundary issues with your employer, keep the bag in or near your workplace or station.

If boundaries once again feel like they're becoming compromised, use your personal judgment how and when to recharge and reenchant the bag so its magick can continue to work in perpetuity.

Keeping Enemies at Bay

Let's be honest; the concept of an enemy is a tough one—it's complicated, convoluted, and can sometimes be rooted in paranoia. Although it's a shorthand way to distinguish those who mean one harm from those who are benevolent, to label a person so harshly is a bit reductive. Sometimes the mind plays tricks, and it's our responsibility as practitioners of magick to question ourselves and to remember that life is full of intricacies. Life is nuanced and there are no absolutes. Not everyone is out to get us, nor us them, thankfully!

Socially, there may be another side to any given story, gossip may be afoot, and sometimes perceived curses and hexes actually originate from within. Assuming one has thought through all possible scenarios and perspectives, if there's someone you're quite certain wishes you harm, follow this spell. You can also perform the spell if you sense external negative energy but are unsure of the origin.

If someone(s) do not actively wish you harm, this working will not have negative effects because its essence is protective—and who couldn't use a bit of protection?

Gather a dead bug outside or at a windowsill (do not kill one for this purpose) and powder its corpse, ideally using a mortar and pestle. Combine this with black salt (see page 171) along with herbs of protection you're familiar with. I recommend wormwood, cloves, nettles, agrimony, and rue.

As you powder, enchant, and eventually store the mixture in a jar, keep repeating the sacred term "elohim" (*ell-oh-heem*) whispered, spoken loudly, *and* said in your mind. This invites divine protection regardless of your personal spiritual proclivities.

With your mixture now pieced and powdered, sprinkle this around your property or the space you wish to gain protection from wickedness. Once sprinkled, the powder should be invisible to the naked eye. As you sprinkle the mixture wherever you see fit, repeat these words as many times as you'd like:

Evil begone: reflected, deflected!
I hereby declare: this space is protected!

A Mirror Ward for Returning to Sender (Guest Spell)

The following spell is written by Kenny Garza (Colt Stagmoon). He and I first connected through the Pagan temple I jointly operated in Missoula, Montana. I'll never forget the Yuletide event where he gifted four gorgeous handmade charms for each of the ritual room's elemental altars. Since then, he has grown in remarkable ways as a Witch, as an artist, and as a quality human being. Enjoy his powerful spell for reflecting and returning negative energy to its source. This style of magick is indeed quite potent!

We all pick up undesirable energy in our daily lives, but not everyone keeps up with their spiritual hygiene. Along with keeping oneself physically and energetically clean, keeping one's home cleansed and protected is equally important. This spell is great to use as a basic ward to bounce negativity that makes its way to your home back to its source, whether it was brought to you intentionally or unintentionally.

Obtain a mirror that has a frame or backing and that can be hung on the wall. The mirror should be relatively small but still big enough to see your face.

On the back of the mirror, draw or paint a protective symbol or sigil, such as the ancient SATOR square. This is a Latin palindrome square used as a charm against evil and bad luck.

S	A	T	O	R
A	R	E	P	O
T	E	N	E	T
O	P	E	R	A
R	O	T	A	S

Next, make an infusion of agrimony, thyme, mugwort, patchouli, and pine, or any other herbs that have protective or reversing qualities. You may also wish to burn what's known as a reversing candle, which can be found in metaphysical stores worldwide.

Wash the surface of the mirror with the herbal infusion and a cloth, visualizing all harmful energy bouncing off of the mirror and returning to its source. As you do so, state the following:

Mirror of reflection,
Assist in this deflection,
Send back any negativity that comes to me,
As I will, so shall it be!

Hang the mirror in a place where it will catch the reflection of the psychic muck that may try to make its way into your home, such as a wall that faces your front door, on the outside of your front door, or in a front-facing window. Refresh the mirror with the herbal infusion and spoken words whenever you feel the need.

Rot Away Wickedness

If you believe wickedness has been either cast toward you or that you've accumulated it heavily as of late in the course of everyday life, try this simple spell.

To the best of your ability, roll a fresh apple all around your body or have a magickal friend assist in doing so. Hold the apple to your mouth and exhale deeply five times, envisioning any astral gunk accumulated on your aura entering the fruit. Each time you inhale, lift your head to look above and visualize pure cleansing, cosmic light entering your body.

Using your athame or kitchen knife (or a marker if you don't trust yourself with sharp objects), carve words and symbols that represent the awful qualities you're commanding to rot away. You'll know what to inscribe.

Once finished, place the apple in a large glass jar (slice the fruit in quarters if needed) and add any combination of the following: angelica root, nettles, cloves, and salt. Finally, add eight cloves of fresh garlic. While adding each clove, state the following. Each line that begins with "wickedness" should be spoken while adding each clove, and the final line spoken after all cloves have been added:

Wickedness from the west,
Wickedness from the north,
Wickedness from the east,
Wickedness from the south,
Wickedness from above,
Wickedness from below,
Wickedness from within,

Wickedness from without,
Begone, rot away, you are unwelcome here,
As I will, so mote it be!

Conclude by spitting forcefully in the jar, sealing it tightly, shaking it up, and tucking it somewhere secret. Cleanse yourself by burning sacred herbs or incense around your body. Allow the jar to sit one or three moon cycles (mark your calendar so you remember), and on that day, simply toss the rotten mixture in the trash.

Averting the Evil Eye

The evil eye is so widely recognized that it's even an emoji! In short, the term "evil eye" may refer both to the condition and to the symbol itself. Recognized throughout cultures near and far, the evil eye is also called the covetous gaze. Despite the name, the energy of covetousness goes far beyond mere jealousy and envy. Those who cast the evil eye intentionally or unintentionally are not only jealous and envious of the fortune of another, but they also wish misfortune and loss upon them. It's a nasty curse, and this is why we see so many charms—traditionally made of glass colored blue, black, and white—to protect one's person and property against such wickedness.

The Hebrew verb *lefargen* and its noun form, *firgun,* refer to a concept of social decorum. To engage in lefargen is "to support, not to envy or begrudge another's success."[11] The

11. Tamar Katriel, "Lefargen: A Study in Israeli Semantics of Social Relations" in *Language and Communication in Israel,* vol IX, eds. Hanna Herzog and Eliezer Ben-Rafael (Routledge, 2001), 31.

wickedness behind an evil eye curse is, in essence, the opposite of lefargen, as those casting the evil eye are motivated by an overwhelming sense of personal injustice in the face of another's success. It all boils down to perception and intention. The ease with which one may cast this curse demonstrates the need to protect against it. One need not sit down and formally cast a vampiric spell in order for the covetous gaze to take hold; simple rumination on covetous thoughts may activate the evil eye.

Charmery and magickal work for combating the evil eye may be preventative as safeguards to ensure ongoing healthy function or curative, reacting after the gaze has taken hold. Charms against the evil eye effectively act as wards, either against what has been placed or which may arise, thus the methodologies listed below may be equally utilized in both scenarios.

An ancient protective and healing symbol recognized around the world is the *Hamsa*, an open five-fingered hand, with fingers pointed upward or downward, often with the Eye of Providence or Eye of Horus depicted in the center of the palm. This symbol holds cultural and religious significance in Judaism and Islam, however, its usage in Middle Eastern cultures predates both organized religions. The word "hamsa" derives from the word for "five" in Arabic (*khamsa*) and Hebrew (*hamesh*), and thus "hamesh hand" and "chamsa" are also recognized monikers for this familiar symbol, all of which bring focus to the five fingers. The number five holds sacred significance to these groups as a reference to the five-book sacred text, the Torah, or books of Moses from which these three monotheistic sister religions grew. The three central fingers represent these sister religions but are also symbolic of virtues for moral behavior: the three primary virtues of wisdom, strength, and beauty and the three grand principles of brotherly love, relief, and truth. In Islam, this symbol is also called the Hand of Fatima, referencing a story about the Prophet Mohammed's daughter.

The Hamsa stops oncoming offenses with a raised hand, palm displayed, and the fingers immediately visible. The fingers are also believed to ward off aggressors and to blind evil. Bringing the fingers together in a sealed presentation brings luck.

The eye in the palm is meant to repel malevolent gazes, such as those initiated by the evil eye. Due to its repellent quality, the eye also appears in tokens called *nazars*. In Hinduism, the word *nazar* refers to the evil eye, stemming from the literal meaning "an unobstructed line of sight," taken from an Arabic root.[12] The nazar tokens may be worn or carried as wards. Because of their widespread recognition, nazars and items featuring the Hamsa hand are widely available for purchase around the world.

Check out Etsy, eBay, and local metaphysical or import shops for protective nazars and Hamsas aplenty! Wear, hang, and incorporate these while doing magick to guard against the covetous gaze or against negative external energy in general.

The following list is both for curiosity and practicality's sakes. Please note that these cross-cultural protective methods are just that: multicultural. It's important for us to consider our own heritage and country of origin or upbringing while respecting those

12. "Nazar" in *The Illustrated Encyclopedia of Hinduism*, vol. 2, edited by James G. Lochtefeld (Rosen Publishing, 2002), 470–71. Via Gale eBooks (accessed May 11, 2025), https://link-gale-com.ezproxy.lib.utexas.edu/apps/doc/CX2536101517/GVRL?u=txshracd2598&sid=bookmark-GVRL&xid=cc3c2c2a.

of others. If you feel some of these practices would be culturally appropriative if you performed them, I advise against doing so. Others, however, are more general, such as wearing black tourmaline. Please conduct further research and reflect upon the phenomenon of cultural appropriation if you feel uncomfortable with any of these methods or other cross-cultural approaches presented in this book.

While performing any of the activities you resonate with and feel comfortable doing, you may wish to repeat the following or something similar:

No longer bombarded,
For I am safeguarded!

- Wear and hang cowrie shells to protect against the evil eye.
- Hang a braid of garlic above your primary entrance; traditionally this knot has twelve full bulbs of garlic.
- Use the stone black tourmaline as a necklace, as a hanging protection charm, or add chips of the stone to protective mixtures.
- When protecting against the evil eye, place both hands in a "mudra" of sorts: the pinkie and pointer finger extended and the others tucked in; this is also called the horned god or rock n' roll symbol.
- Wear eyeliner, visualizing protection while applying it; particularly effective is black kohl, specifically the Ayurvedic eyeliner *kajal*, which is used in India and the Middle East to protect against the evil eye, where it is especially applied to children's eyes for this purpose.

- Anoint the afflicted person with juniper oil until the condition resolves itself.
- The henna plant—particularly when dried, powdered, and used as a temporary tattoo paste called *mehndi* as well as a natural hair dye, has been renowned everywhere from ancient Egypt to modern India to bring about blessings while simultaneously warding off negative energy and the covetous gaze.
- To a few cups of warm water, add a square or ball of blue añil (also known as bluestone, blue vitriol, or "bluing" in Hoodoo) with a pinch or square of camphor (a resin commonly used in Hindu worship) and a handful of sea salt. Sprinkle or spray this mixture around the house for ongoing protection against the evil eye and negative external energies in general.
- Burn sage in any ritual to protect against the covetous gaze.
- Pour a libation of beer and rub the afflicted with bread. Do not consume either!
- An herb renowned to help remove curses of any type is hyssop. In a bath, combine equal parts Epsom salt, Himalayan salt, and baking soda, followed by a few droppers-full of hyssop tincture or extract and a bit of your favorite essential oil.
- To amplify any of the above, a popular Hoodoo remedy against the evil eye is to simply carry a sachet consisting of the herbs anise, rue, and agrimony. Add black pepper and black tourmaline for an extra sock-it-to-'em.

Protecting Your Animal Familiar

If we're gonna protect ourselves, it's a good idea to protect our animal allies in the process. Although we humans are animals ourselves—and many theories state that our genetics may be a little *more* than just mammalian—our nonhuman animal comrades hold a special place in the heart of nature-based mystics.

Those who love and work with nature often report feeling an emotional bond with animals, especially our pets. For all intents and purposes, pets are our familiars. Some Witches and magickal folk work with invisible familiars or animal oversouls, but many of us enjoy a distinct and magickal bond with the physical animals we care for—and who care for us. Pets are unconditionally loving friends; they are family who enrich our lives and gift us with a magickal presence (and entertainment!) unmatched by any human.

Much like the word "Witch," "familiar" is something that modern practitioners have reclaimed, as both words have carried connotations of evildoing throughout points in human history and still do in some cultures. "Familiar" comes from the Latin *familiaris,* referring to someone or something belonging to a household, such as a servant.[13] During medieval Christian Europe's Burning Times, for example, pets belonging to accused Witches as well as countless innocent feral animals were themselves accused of being shape-shifting demons, especially cats, and most especially black cats. Many cultures are still superstitious and behave horrifically to black cats and other animals to this day.

In Hawaiian culture, the term *kahu* means "protector" or "guardian" of something sacred or precious, and is applied to pets,

13. Merriam-Webster.com Dictionary, s.v. "familiar," accessed April 23, 2025, https://www.merriam-webster.com/dictionary/familiar.

children, the land, and other aspects of life.[14] This is the spiritual duty we take as humans with our beloved animal kindred. Even with the awareness that we are likely to accompany our pets until their fated dying day, that inevitable pain is worth every beautiful moment of loving companionship.

In addition to action on physical plane, such as spaying, neutering, microchipping, sheltering, loving, and giving quality food, we can take a few mystical steps to bond with and protect our animal allies. Begin by lighting a brown candle of any size; brown provides a direct link to the animal realm and can be used in any magick associated with animals.

Ideally within a greater ritual procedure, use a sterile lancet to draw a single drop of blood from the ring finger of each hand. Take your pet's favorite edible treats and anoint them with your blood. As you do, focus on the love you feel for your pet or pets, allowing gratitude to permeate your mind and enter the food by way of your skin's puncture. Feed this offering to your familiar in order to dedicate and strengthen your timeless bond.

Please note that you should *not* feed these drops of your own blood to your pet if you are currently sick or have a blood-borne illness: What are known as reverse zoonoses—illness transmitted to animals from humans—is always a possibility, though it is rare. Influenza, tuberculosis, MRSA, ringworm, mumps, and SARS-CoV-2 (the virus that causes COVID-19) are examples of illnesses that are capable of being transmitted from humans to animals. In other words, be smart. If there is any doubt, use a little bit of saliva instead or, if you're extra cautious, simply infuse the treats with your own energy by performing a bit of intuitive energy work.

---

14. Cecilio Blanco Ledesma, "Kahu," *Medium* (blog) August 8, 2023, https://medium.com/@cecilledesma_20547/kahu-ae37d36358ee.

Ceremonially dedicate a mixture of herbs to protect your familiar by blending Saint John's wort, marshmallow root, and clovers, all of which have been used historically for protecting animals. You may choose to hang these herbs in a bag where they slumber or surround some of their essence (fur, feathers, sheds, etc.) with this mixture upon a dedicated altar.

Finally, get their bowl of drinking water and, after thoroughly cleaning the bowl and refreshing it with pure water, use the pointer finger of your right hand to write blessings upon the water's surface, one letter at a time. Once consumed, your familiar will be filled with the protective and grateful intentions you've intended.

For an additional boost of magickal bonding and protection, purchase and ceremonially bless high-quality animal food, wet and dry, before gifting it as an offering to your local animal shelters.

CHAPTER 5

Removing & Refreshing

As explored previously, there are times in which we accumulate external shadowy energy in daily life. This external energy plays with our *own* shadows, and sometimes it's challenging to discern where these energies originate. For that reason, removing dark energy of the harmful variety is essential, especially if we feel off-kilter and have a hunch that what we're feeling is not entirely internal.

Being the central chapter of the section focused on interpersonal shadow work, the goal is just that: coming back to center. This chapter begins with a curse removal bathing spell and moves into other types of removal magick such as cord cutting, recovering from exhaustion, and banishing potentially harmful energy that could have been picked up in day-to-day life.

It's important to replace energies we've cast away with something different in its place. For this reason, the refreshing aspect is of great importance. The entries focused on this side of the equation focus on the magick of glamoury, personal vows, and self-dedication. This chapter may also inspire you to create your own creative spells, charms, and rituals aimed at removing harmful shadows and invoking healthier energy in their place.

A Curse Removal Bath

Bathing is one of the most common methods of removing curses, hexes, jinxes, and negativities originating from outside sources. If you believe you've been intentionally or unintentionally cursed, taking a magickal cleansing bath is a good idea.

Remember to modify and tailor this spell or any other to fit your condition. If you don't have access to a bathtub, modify the bath bag to become a single-use shower squeeze. If you don't have access to all the ingredients, use what you can. These suggestions reflect my research into cleansing baths across various cultures and times, so make it your own and enjoy the magickal refreshment.

Using a drawstring muslin bag or something similarly all-natural, place a combination of any the following herbs within: hyssop, rue, agrimony, poke root, angelica root, annatto, nettles, and juniper. Additionally, cut a lemon in quarters and place it in the bathwater. You may also wish to add a can of beer, a classic ingredient in purification soaks.

When drawing the bath, use your finger to draw pentagrams on the water's surface. Instead of adding caustic ammonia to the water (a common practice in Hoodoo), add a splash of vinegar and/or witch hazel astringent. Alternatively, you can put a little bit of your own urine in the tub or pee a wee bit while you're in there—I know it sounds gross, but the principle is the same. Urine also represents the removal of toxins because that's its purpose in the body, and also represents protective boundaries—marking one's territory.

Add at least one cup of sea salt and stir the warm water in a widdershins (counterclockwise) fashion, softly repeating the words "curses, hexes, and bad juju removed."

If you wish to burn a curse-removing incense mixture in the bathroom, combine dragon's blood resin with a little valerian root, agrimony, and/or wood betony, all of which have curse-removing properties when burned. This mixture should, of course, be burned safely on a designated incense charcoal disk and in a fireproof dish or burner.

Meditate in the water and fully submerge a number of times. Speak your personal wishes and prayers for removing nasty energy that's entered your sphere. Once the water has turned lukewarm, drain the tub and allow your body to air dry rather than using a towel.

Conclude by burning sacred herbs or incense around your body, and use your intention to visualize protective, balancing energy entering your sphere from above (Father Sky) and below (Mother Earth). Fill your body with positive, protective energy however you see fit, and be sure to thank your spirit guides and the Powers That Be.

Traditional Cord Cutting

Cord cutting is a form of shadow work because it implies recognizing and choosing to release toxic ties with another person, situation, occupation, or something else that is no longer a mutually beneficial or uplifting relationship.

If you've decided that your connection to something or someone has reached a point deserving of severance, perform this spell in conjunction with "real world" activity to separate yourself from the other. You should be firmly resolved in this decision, as spells like this are powerful and should not be approached lightly.

Use your creativity and intuition to create something that represents the person, people, or situation you are decidedly separating from your life. This could be anything from handwriting to a drawing, from clothing to a print-out.

On the night of a full or waning moon, light a black candle to signify the end of a connection. Have your athame or a pair of scissors within reach. Wrap string, yarn, or twine around the item that represents the other, and wrap the remaining end around your body, ensuring there is a length of cord between you. Gazing at the item you've bound, state in a loud voice:

This represents [name of person] *and the connection between us.*
I hereby sever our connection, which has become unhealthy.
Overseen by the guides, gods, and guardians, I now cut all ties.

Blur your vision to see the cord between you filled with a combination of your energy and that of the other. See how the two energies mix and intermingle. When you're ready, cut the physical cord between you with a loud "Heh!" or similar vocalization. Visualize their energy instantly returning to them, and your own energy swiftly returning to your body. Hold your right hand to your heart and your left hand toward the other in a "talk to the hand" position. Conclude by loudly stating, "And so it is done!"

Cut the cord into numerous sections and burn or throw it away. Do the same with the item representing the other, or whatever feels most appropriate. Keep in mind that if your mind continues to wander over time to a place of doubt and uncertainty regarding the cord cutting, it disempowers the spell and may allow those ties to return on an unwanted level. Be resolute in your decision with magick like this!

Softening Cruel Hearts & Minds

Sometimes it's difficult to understand how some people can be profoundly cruel, controlling, vindictive, selfish, sadistic, or just plain evil. Whether it's the politician who exploits the vulnerable or the spiteful landlord on a power trip, self-serving cruelty is an ongoing epidemic in a world that's equally as capable of creating heavenly conditions for all.

Empathy, sympathy, and compassion don't come naturally to everyone, and sometimes it can seem like there's nothing we can do about it. Although education is profoundly important in helping inspire change, if a person legitimately doesn't give a shit about the welfare of others, that sort of mental conditioning and sickness is not something we're capable of curing. We can, however, lend a bit of magick... or a lot.

To help soften the minds and hearts of those who engage in wanton cruelty, either put their image directly in your mind's eye or gaze upon a picture or video of the individual. Take some time to visualize their heart chakra (*anahata*) growing, opening, and glowing in tones of green, kind of like the Grinch's heart growing in size.

Do the same with their brow or third-eye chakra (*ajna*), but visualize it growing and swirling in hues of violet and indigo. Next, see a cord connecting these two chakra points, the colors intermingling to form a teal-toned link from mind to heart. As you visualize their growing compassion (heart) with their ability to see the error of their ways (brow), repeat the Sanskrit names of each chakra multiple times:

Ajna, anahata, grow, grow, grow.

Repeat for as long as you feel guided and conclude by sending a large blast of light with your final exhale. Stop looking at their image for now, knowing that you've done an act of good by working with their shadow, far exceeding mere "thoughts and prayers."

If creating a more intricate, artistic spell of this nature, consider affixing a green jasper stone to the heart of their image, as it's believed to promote and encourage empathy. The most relevant herbs you may wish to incorporate for this purpose include lavender, rose, and balm of Gilead (buds of the poplar tree).

Out with the Sucky, In with the Lucky

If you've been feeling particularly misunderstood lately or have experienced negative social interactions that seemed to paint an unfair picture of your character, this spell may be beneficial.

People who are energetically and emotionally sensitive will often hold difficult experiences in their sphere of energy. When ongoing or chronic, this clutching of negativity can manifest as illnesses or mental health struggles. A simple way to quickly cleanse energy before it builds up is to use two of the most common ingredients in the book: sugar and salt.

Go outside with a small bowl of powdered confectioner's sugar and another of salt, whether it's regular rock salt, Himalayan pink salt, or black salt (see page 171). Take some deep breaths and sense the energy stuck in your field. When you're ready, sprinkle most of the salt over your body, envisioning the salt capturing and grounding the energy. Sprinkle the remainder of the salt in a circle around your body.

Grabbing the bowl of powdered sugar, place a small amount in your right hand and, starting in the east and ending in the north, blow sugar from your hand toward each direction, stating the following each time:

Sweetness around, sweetness abound!

Finish by envisioning your body surrounded in sweet sparkles of light. You may wish to further envision the energetic ick further entering the earth and dissolving back to nature. Conclude the spell by eating a molasses cookie or a spoonful of molasses, which is believed to invoke goodness in place of darkness.

Banishing Accumulated Vibes

It's normal to accumulate foreign energy after interacting with the public. For those of us who are more sensitive and who may have our guard down when engaging socially, it's good practice to release these energetic accumulations on a regular basis. This is one method.

Take a fresh egg, ideally cage-free and organic (even better if it's from a local black-feathered hen), and use a needle to make small holes on the top and bottom. Blow out the egg into a bowl; if you find this challenging, look up egg blowing online to discover tips and tricks.

With the fragile hollow egg in hand, use a black marker to write words and symbols representing all the things you're worried about having accumulated socially. Consider your recent environments and any negative interactions you may have recently experienced. Once finished, "rub" the hollow egg on your aura, envisioning those qualities filling up the shell. Conclude by taking a handful of salt in your right hand, place the hollow egg on top, and forcefully say "begone!" while crushing it to pieces.

Throw the egg and salt in the trash, wash your hands, and cleanse your energy field however you see fit. Make scrambled eggs with the yolk and white that you blew out—because it wasn't used in the spell, it is fresh and untainted. You could also use it in baking or cooking if you have a proclivity toward Kitchen Witchery.

Casting Off Social Muck

Depending on one's level of sensitivity, spending a significant amount of time in public requires a bit of solitude to counteract social overload. For some, a plain ol' trip to the grocery store can be an overwhelming experience (even *with* pre-constructed energetic shields), while others may feel energetically overloaded after a night out on the town. Whatever the scenario, it's not impossible to get energetically "slimed" out in public. The chances increase, however, when people are exhibiting strong emotions around you... or there's a lot of drinking going on! If you've found your mood inexplicably shifting toward the pessimistic or anxious after some time in public, perform this spell to help refresh your energy.

Take a hot shower with high water pressure. Bring a large handful of salt into the shower to wash around your body to aid the cleansing process. After showering off, get an edible member of the nightshade family such as a tomato, eggplant, or potato. (Yes, you can use French fries in a pinch!) Ingesting an edible nightshade helps with banishing and releasing accumulated energy, a well-known power of Solanaceae plants. The food itself is also filling, making this a dual-action spell.

Prepare the item to eat, finishing with a sprinkle of salt. Hold your hands above it and, before consuming, see it glowing in every color of the rainbow, thereby linking its cleansing energy to all your chakras. Hold the food toward the sky, toward the earth, and to all four directions. As you eat, see its energy replacing socially-accumulated muck with balancing fulfillment. For added power, burn rosemary around your body to disperse energy you may have unintentionally collected.

Recovering from Social Exhaustion

There's no easy fix for the fatigue, listlessness, and discomfort that arise from feelings of exhaustion. There are root causes, however, and we all deserve to understand them in an act of self-knowledge and respect.

Are you burning the candle at both ends while struggling to survive? Are you taking on too many obligations or ruminating with mental gymnastics? Is there unaddressed depression that's begging for attention beneath the surface? Are you on a new medication or supplement? Have you recently changed something about your diet or routine?

Maybe what you're feeling is social and not entirely personal. Many sensitive, psychic, empathic, and mystical folks demonstrate a greater state of overwhelm in the face of sociopolitical stress. Global and national violations of human rights, animal rights, and the exploitation of natural resources are understandable reasons for feeling mental, emotional, and spiritual exhaustion. We can only do what we can do, and any step in the right direction echoes forth.

For many sensitive folks, even the most positive and upbeat public interactions can feel draining at times. Feeling this way is a sign to pay attention to the body and mind, and to replenish your energetic reserves before socially reengaging too heavily.

If you're feeling exhausted by society, try this ten-hour spell. Begin by making a list, one through ten. Ten is the number for

Malkuth on the esoteric Tree of Life and is ruled by Earth as a planet. Therefore, incorporate a circled cross somewhere in this working, the symbol for planet Earth (see previous page).

Take some time to reflect on what you're feeling. Clear your mind and ask the assistance of your spiritual guides and higher self. Create a list of ten different activities you can do throughout the course of a day to aid in your energetic recovery. Each number represents a different hour of the day. Plan this day accordingly. If you're able to be solitary or mostly alone throughout these ten hours, great. If you need to schedule around obligations, modify as you see fit. The items on your list should consist of simple, creative activities you can perform each hour. For example: "Hour 1: 9 a.m.–Salt scrub in the shower; Hour 2: 10 a.m.–Yoga for 20 minutes; Hour 3: 11 a.m.–Walk around the block and invoke sunlight," and so on.

Reflect on the day for which you're planning this rejuvenating regimen, and be sure to think outside the box. Maybe you'll designate jump-roping in the afternoon or singing in the evening. You could begin a piece of art when you wake up or choose to work with the elements or start reading a novel before winding down at night. Have fun planning, and hold yourself to it. Keep in mind that any given activity does not need to take up a full hour; these are meant to be a series of engaging, refreshing activities that focus on personal health, wellness, and inspiration. Each step should help reset and ground your energy in an effort to power through the shadow of social exhaustion.

Set your phone or another timer to go off each hour, beginning on the first of the ten hours you've set. This will be a day of personal dedication and self-discipline for your own necessary benefit.

At the top of each hour, go to your altar or a designated spot to reaffirm your day's dedication. Determine if you'd like to do a ritualistic activity each time, such as lighting a candle for a few minutes, a brief meditation, holding an empowered gemstone, or even something routine like taking a sip of kombucha.

Declare the following words at the top of each hour, following each statement by stating the activity you have planned:

By hour of one, this spell has begun.
By hour of two, I'm empowered through and through.
By hour of three, my energy returns to me.
By hour of four, exhaustion is no more.
By hour of five, my will is to thrive.
By hour of six, my balance is fixed.
By hour of seven, my power awakens.
By hour of eight, rejuvenation I mandate.
By hour of nine, inspiration is mine.
By hour of ten, I find healing again.

Enjoy your day of refreshment, restoration, and empowerment to help equip you with the strength to conquer life's social necessities.

Dark Makeup for Glamoury

Makeup and face paint have been used ceremonially since the dawn of humanity. Glamoury, or glamour magick, takes many forms and can be used for many reasons. If you wish to explore this subject deeper, I recommend books written by my wise and fabulous friend Michael Herkes, the Glam Witch.

Makeup can be an excellent component of magickal work for a variety of purposes. When performing shadow magick, whether solitary or in public, dark makeup is the logical go-to. If makeup is your thing, consider enchanting dark palettes, lipsticks, eyeliners, mascaras, and so on. All-natural makeup is more effective due to the microplastics and chemicals found in cheaper cosmetics.

Consider your purpose for enchanting the makeup. Maybe it's to add a layer of protection, maybe it's to bond with unseen energy, maybe to garner the attention of a desirable individual—the list goes on. Place the makeup in a bowl on your lap.

While sitting in a comfortable position, take some deep breaths and visualize the items glowing in colors associated with your intention. Pass each item through an element, such as salt for earth, a candle flame for fire, incense for air, and a drop of water for water. As you do so, state your intention or intentions:

This dark makeup I enchant
by the element ______ in order to ______.

Place the makeup either outside or on a windowsill for twenty-four hours before using so that it can soak up a full day's turn of moonlight and sunlight. For an added boost, perform this enchantment on the evening of a full moon.

A Charm for Healers

Professions and practices focused on healing on any level are very much related to shadow work. To invite healing is to acknowledge that which is imbalanced, the term "healing" itself implies that something is off-kilter and needs rebalancing. If you work in a healing profession—anything from massage therapy to counseling to sound healing—it's wise to keep a magickal pouch in your office or workspace. The pouch can be a drawstring sachet, a little pillow you've stitched, a fixed gris-gris mojo bag, or even a little glass jar for good vibes. Just try to avoid plastic materials in any spiritual working.

Draw an open eye on your charm bag to represent your ability to see each client's needs. On the reverse, draw a pentagram inside a square with your signature in the middle of the symbol to represent you being protected throughout your work.

Add items to the bag for insight and clarity, namely the stone tiger's eye and the herb eyebright. Add herbs, stones, and other materials tailored to your field of healing work. For example, you may add seashells if the work you do focuses on deep emotional processing. You could include dried flower petals and amethyst if you're a relationship coach. Yarrow, wormwood, and amethyst would be good to include if you're an addictions counselor. The options are endless and entirely rely on your intuition and creativity.

Once finalized, seal the bag or jar with a kiss. Hold it to the ground, to your heart, and then to the sky. Declare:

My calling in life is to help others heal.
With protection and insight, this charm makes it real!

A Black Sheep's Dedication

Who wants to be normal? Not me! The norm is often boring and lackluster, and those of us who live and think outside the box (as long as no one's getting harmed) deserve to be confident in ourselves. Diversity makes the world go 'round! This dedication helps invoke confidence and may be repeated when the world's got you down.

In a sacred space on a new or dark moon, anoint a black candle with your favorite essential oil (or van van) after carving all your names in the wax. By "all your names," I mean your full birth name, common name, nicknames, and so on. Dress yourself in all black and either wear or carry a stone of citrine or carnelian for self-empowerment.

Take a number of deep, grounding breaths and declare:

Powers That be, now take heed, for I am unique in thought and deed.
My uniqueness is a virtue, my presence is a power,
I bless and give blessings every day and every hour.
I accept and honor my test of standing out from the rest.
Joy in myself I now have awoke,
and sight of my purpose I hereby invoke!

Preparing for a Social Media Break

Social media is a tricky beast. Like any tool in life, we can use our socials to connect with others instantly or to learn information about the world, literally at our fingertips! On the other hand, socials offer a platform for bullying, trolling, and harassment. Social media can offer our brains happy hits of dopamine if used in moderation just as it can become an addictive experience similar to gambling or video game dependencies.

If you know it's time to take a break from social media for some amount of time, whether for a couple days or a couple months, place your electronics in front of you inside a temporary circle made of salt and the herb yarrow for boundaries. (You can remove them from this circle for non-social media use afterward.) An ideal time to do this is during a Mercury retrograde, or when the sun or moon is in a sign ruled by Mercury (Gemini or Virgo).

Use your pointer finger to draw the symbol for Mercury on top of each device (previous page). Gaze at the items and speak:

Mercurial tech, how I honor your gifts,
But from social media I now must shift.
When balance is had, I'll return to the web,
At present my focus is elsewhere instead.

Preparing for a Vow of Silence

In Sanskrit, the devotional period of voluntary silence is called *mauna vrat, mauna* means "silence" and *vrat* (or *vratra*) means "vow." These vows are also found outside of Hindu and Vedic religions, each with a different purpose. To practice silence is to connect with shadow, assisting the devotee in focusing inward and learning the true power of spoken word.

A vow of silence is a form of fasting and can have interesting social effects. I once had a coven member go hardcore in their devotions by performing a vow of silence for a year and a day; their life was positively transformed as a result! For a lengthy exploration into the power of fasting, please check out my book *A Witch's Shadow Magick Compendium*.

In meditation, decide on the length of your vow. It may be only for a day, for three days, for a lunar cycle, or even longer. From your occupation to your family, there are numerous factors to consider; a vow of this kind *will* affect your social life in some manner. You'll also want to decide whether you are fasting from speech alone or extending it to include virtual communication, texting, and handwriting.

Prepare a notecard to carry with you that easily states why you cannot talk. You can show this piece of paper to anyone who wasn't previously made aware of your dedication. I recommend something simple such as, "Vow of silence! :) I can speak again on [insert day]."

Prepare your final words to speak at this time as you think about any meaningful words of power with which you can break the vow of silence when the time comes. Hold the notecard to your heart, face the east, and speak your dedication:

For _____ days I invoke this vow,
These words are the last I speak for now.
Quietude becomes a divine affirmation,
This vow of silence is my dedication.
I now look inward to see and to know,
And by this vow I spiritually grow!
Shhhhhh …

CHAPTER 6

Navigating Society

We humans are social creatures. Navigating the ups and downs of society is hard work, and we need to keep both protected and aware of the world around us.

This is the chapter that contains alternatives to cursing, hexing, and binding. Because we must remain steadfastly wise in our work, it's important to be mindful of the karmic implications of our magick. Our magickal work is ideally a reflection and an extension of how we operate on a daily basis. Our magick is a reflection of our morals. If someone has been harassing or trying to harm you metaphysically (up to and including the general energy they project toward you in daily life), these mindful cursing alternatives can be of great benefit and are wonderful examples of how shadow magick may be worked for the greater good. We *all* deserve to be safe.

In this chapter focused on social interaction, you'll naturally find spells focused on mending disagreements, stopping gossip, and overcoming public scrutiny. You'll also find spells for purposes such as social invisibility, ambient energy feeding, and a few unlikely surprises along the way!

This chapter also contains workings focused on helping others through their own shadows, including spells centered on activism and remote healing. As responsible spellcasters, it's our duty to help ourselves first and then assist others to the best of our ability.

Relieving Social Anxiety

Social anxiety is an incredibly common occurrence for reasons far too vast to explore here. A great many people suffer from anxiety conditions or disorders, which is perfectly understandable (within reason) considering the state of the world and human behavior in general.

A spell for relieving this type of anxiety can certainly help alongside professional assistance (please see this book's opening disclaimer on page xi, just before the table of contents) and can also be used when those anxious feelings seem stronger than they do in everyday functioning.

Procure a small amount of the hottest fresh peppers you can find. (Substitute a handful of dried crushed red pepper or black pepper if needed.) Cup these peppers in your hand and shake them around your body, especially around the belly and head.

As you agitate the peppers in this manner, envision your social anxiety "zapping" the peppers, entering them forcefully to be captured within. State your intention in your own words as you do this, for example, "Social anxiety now enters these peppers."

Go outside away from prying eyes, and either throw the peppers far away *or* bury them in a hole. As you do this, simply declare "Anxiety begone!"

Sprinkle salt where you threw or buried the peppers, return home, and scrub your hands with salted water. Splash your face with the water and anoint both your head and belly to aid in protection. Take deep breaths and cleanse your energy in whatever manner feels right.

For an added boost, include jasmine flowers in some way, such as a tea or in a warm bath. Jasmine carries metaphysical qualities of relieving anxiety, particularly of the social variety.

Calming Public Speaking Anxiety

One of people's highest-ranking fears in study after study is public speaking. If you're one of these people and find yourself in a situation that requires public speaking, try this spell. Whether you're preparing for a school presentation, a work conference, an interview, or a group that requires everyone to introduce themselves, this magickal work can aid in preparation. However, for anxiety that is debilitating, consider inquiring with a physician about medications that can specifically target public speaking anxiety such as a beta-blocker or low-dose benzodiazepine.

Get a bowl of birdseed or something that birds will consume, such as shelled peanuts, sunflower seeds, or dried rice. Contrary to popular belief, birds can and do eat rice without exploding!

In a location birds frequent, enter a peaceful state of mind with the offering bowl in hand. Close your eyes, take deep breaths, and calm your heart rate. Think about the upcoming presentation or whatever is causing anxiety. Visualize the occurrence going well, and smile as you toss handfuls of birdseed or the offering you've chosen. Each time anxiety flares up in meditation, take a deep breath and toss another handful.

Before offering the last of it, open your eyes and confidently state:

Avian creatures and birds that fly high,
I implore sacred bonding between you and I.
Your swiftness in flight and song I address,
So my communications will also be blessed.
With each grain you eat, my old fears abate,
So my public speaking is effortlessly great!

Private & Public Anchoring

Sometimes it's hard to leave the house. If you find that anxiety takes over too frequently or too strongly in the face of public obligation (grocery shopping, going to work, and other survival necessities), try carrying a magickal item that links back to the safety of house and home. A simple spell for inviting comforting "home" energy when you're out in public involves creating an energetic anchor.

The most highly magnetic mineral is called magnetite, commonly known as lodestone. This stone is used frequently in magick aimed at attracting and drawing certain energies to the caster and can also be used as an anchoring device.

Acquire two pieces of lodestone and store them together in a piece of natural fabric. After cleansing the bundle with purifying smoke, rub it all around your home to absorb the pleasant, comforting energy of your home. Focus on comforting locations: the bed, your favorite chair, your altar, and most certainly your beloved pets! Please note that if lodestone is unavailable, a suitable substitute for this spell's intentions are two pieces of hematite, ideally raw and unpolished.

Do this regularly to recharge the stones and keep them wrapped on your altar or another special place. When you leave the house, carry one of the lodestones and return it to its partner once you've returned. When social anxiety arises in public, secretly hold the stone and visualize it linking back to the comforting energies of your safe, cozy, and comforting home-base.

Releasing Public Scrutiny

Humans can be viciously cruel. If you've recently been on the receiving end of social judgment whether in person or online, it's good to use a bit of magick to help release and transform those vibes before they take up too much space in your head.

On a few dried bay leaves, use a black marker to write a word or short phrase that expresses how the scrutiny has left you feeling. Examples include "judged," "patronized," "disheartened," and so on.

On the flip side of each bay leaf, draw a large X to indicate banishing and releasing. With a black or white candle lit, go outside and carefully burn each leaf and place their ashes in a container with the herbs mullein and agrimony.

Under cloak of night, deposit this mixture at an intersection that sees heavy traffic in the daytime; this helps disperse the energy and send it away for good!

Halting Slanderous Words

Gossip sucks, backbiting hurts, and nobody is immune to it. We are social creatures, so it's normal to talk about other people *to* other people. There's no harm in chatting if it's not at someone else's expense. However, if you're aware that someone has been unfairly smearing your social image, some anti-gossip magick can be of assistance.

This spell can also be used against a gaslighter (someone trying to make you doubt your sense of reality), a sociopath (someone with no regard for others' feelings), and someone with Narcissistic Personality Disorder (NPD). These personality types all exhibit extreme self-esteem issues that cause them to belittle others in order to feel a sense of superiority. In general, it's worth it to remove these people from your life no matter what it takes; life is too short to endure emotional abuse! I speak from years of experience.

In a ritualistic setting, write the person's name on a large, fresh leaf that resembles a tongue. While binding up the "tongue" with red or black thread, state the following eight times:

[Name of person], *your tongue is now tied.*
Your lies, gossip, and rumors now shrivel and die!

If you don't know the name of the backbiter, say "gossiper" instead.

Roll up this tied tongue and place it in a small drawstring bag with any combination of the following herbs renowned for halting gossip: slippery elm, cloves, chia seeds, lobelia, violet, and mullein. Alternatively or additionally, you can use the old Hoodoo trick of placing the bound tongue in a bag of tobacco mixed with alum powder (or substitute baking powder).

Hang the bag outside near your front door *or* somewhere it will interact with the wind; this connects to the element air, which rules communication.

Trapping Narcissistic Harm (Guest Spell)

The following spell is written by Rahjeena Drabarni. We met through mutual friends on social media, quickly realizing that we had a great deal in common. Being both a survivor of narcissistic abuse and a Romani Arli Witch, Rahjeena has dedicated her life to counseling, educating, and empowering those who have been abused. Feel free to visit her and learn more about her services at https://rahjeena.wixsite.com/mysite.

Personality disorders are grouped into three clusters. Narcissistic Personality Disorder (NPD) falls into cluster B, along with borderline, histrionic, and antisocial disorders. This cluster also encompasses both sociopathy and psychopathy. Sociopathic behaviors display more emotional dysregulation, while psychopathic disorders display less emotional affect.

Not all narcissists are sociopathic, but all sociopaths are narcissistic. The narcissist crosses the line into sociopathy when they display disregard for others, manipulation, and illegal behaviors. An online search can provide education on characteristics and variations that occur in all personality disorders.

People can be toxic without being narcissistic. Don't make the mistake of labeling everyone who doesn't agree with you or is occasionally off-character as being a narcissist. Also, narcissism is on a spectrum. People can intermittently display narcissistic traits, but that doesn't mean they have NPD; only a licensed psychiatrist or clinical psychologist can diagnose this condition.

Energetically, narcissists are energy vampires who thrive on provoking positive or negative emotional reactions. Fear and insecurity rule the narcissist. The need to feel superior and in control results in behavioral patterns aimed at bringing down others' vibrations. Unable to raise their own vibration, narcissists are pathologically envious of others' light and shine.

After thirty-five years as a professional practitioner, spellcasting for myself and clients, I concluded that spellcraft aimed *toward* someone with a personality disorder doesn't really "stick"; it requires constant repetition. I experienced the same with spellcasting involving addicts and with those who have untreated mental disorders. After much trial and error, meticulous note taking, patience, and time, I created some alternate techniques that work proficiently.

This is not a return-to-sender spell, and while it's not innocuous, it is not a curse or hex. If the narcissist stops targeting you, they will not receive consequences. However, they'll still have to contend with the energetic return of their own making.

If your narcissist is harassing, stalking, or currently lives with you, I recommend using the law and courts alongside personal therapy or coaching to help separate them as much as possible from your life. If you lack patience for the long game of this spell, consider hiring a professional practitioner with experience casting against narcissists using stronger and faster means.

This spell consists of sigil creation. If you're unfamiliar, books and articles about sigilry are widely available.

On a Saturday nearest to the dark moon, consult a planetary table to choose the hour of Saturn in your time zone. At your chosen time, clap your hands in all directions, beginning and ending in the west. This both activates your energy and cleanses the space. Follow by using any method of protection from your personal practices.

Mirrors can be made into traps for entities, spirits, and energies. Take a dual-sided handheld *or* compact magnifying makeup mirror that has one magnified mirror and one at regular scale. Pass the open mirror through frankincense smoke.

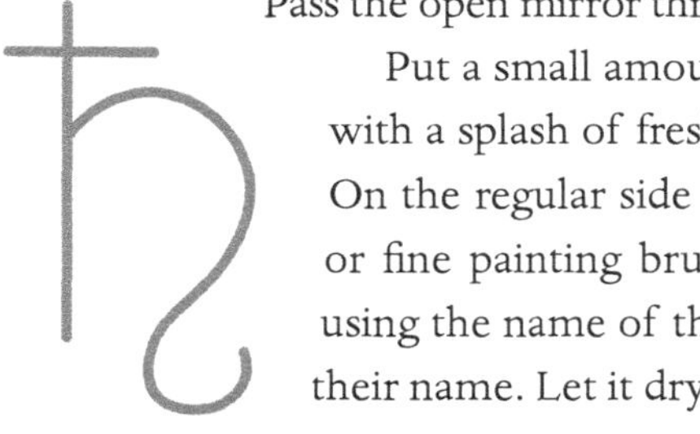

Put a small amount of white vinegar in a bowl with a splash of fresh water to act as invisible ink. On the regular side of the mirror, use a quill pen or fine painting brush to create an invisible sigil using the name of the perpetrator or simply write their name. Let it dry.

Next, *on top* of the previous sigil, superimpose another sigil whose purpose is to command and trap baneful energy sent to you or your loved ones. Alternatively, draw eight arrows pointed inward toward the mirror's center.

While it's drying, focus strongly and say three times:

All baneful energy sent my way,
is trapped in this mirror both night and day.
Each time sent, it shall remain,
instantly transmuted for my gain.
As [name of person] *continues harming me,*
the weaker they become; so mote it be!

Once again, on top of the two invisible sigils on the regular side of the mirror, superimpose a third seal or sigil related to a spirit or deity you have a connection with. Alternately, simply draw the symbol for the planet Saturn (see previous page).

On top of these three invisible symbols, use a photo of the narcissist found online and printed out, or a physical item that has a link to them. Adhere this to the mirror overtop the dried symbols. If you must remain undetected due to safety reasons, take some time to strongly visualize their face instead.

On the magnified side of the mirror, draw a sigil of your name using a black fine-tip permanent marker or just write your initials. Superimpose this with a second black sigil whose purpose is to command the trapped energy to be transmuted into positive, beneficial energy for you to use at will. If you'd rather draw a symbol, draw a deosil (clockwise) spiral beginning at the mirror's magnifying center and spiraling to its edges. Note that in the case of using a permanent marker, you may opt instead to use the vinegar if you need to remain inconspicuous.

When completed, focus strongly and say three times:

Whenever [name of person] *sends an attack,*
their harmful energy is hereby trapped.
All cruel energy is transmuted for my benefit,
to extract and enjoy whenever I see fit.
And so it is!

On the same (magnified) side of the mirror, repeat the third step of the regular side of the mirror: draw the same seal or sigil related to a spirit or deity you have a connection with *or* the symbol for Saturn (page 132). Again, black marker is preferable, but vinegar is okay to use if you don't want anyone else to see it.

Seal the spell by connecting your own energy to the magnified side of the mirror. Exhale onto the surface and anoint its center with your spit and/or a drop of blood. Now it is charged! Thank your spirits; the spell is now set into motion.

Place the mirror at your bedside or under your bed. Recharge the mirror monthly on the last Saturday before the dark moon by feeding the magnified side with your breath, spit, or blood.

If you wish to discontinue the spell, simply stop recharging it monthly; the spell will slowly dissipate. To end it quickly, smash the mirror inside a paper bag outdoors, and throw it into a public trashcan.

Approaching a Confrontation

For some, confrontations, arguments, and miscommunications can be discombobulating, stressful, and emotionally draining. The human experience requires that we confront or be confronted from time to time, and there's nothing inherently wrong with that. What matters is the *approach* of the person who is doing the confrontation; is it occurring out of respect and with a goal of resolution, or is it coming from a place of prejudice and cruelty?

Regardless of details, if you are preparing to confront someone *or* someone you know has said "we need to talk," this spell can help you prepare. Confrontations do not need to become conflicts.

Wear a necklace with a pendant made of black stone such as onyx, obsidian, or black tourmaline. If the confrontation will take place virtually or remotely, smoky quartz is also beneficial. Meditate in a sacred space and take long, slow breaths. Hold your breath for a few moments and exhale slowly a number of times.

Envision the stone's energy growing, glowing, and surrounding your body in an etheric shield. In your own words, ask your spiritual guides for assistance both with accurate communication and energetic protection.

Stand up, place your hands in the *anjali* mudra (prayer hands), and bow to each of the four directions. Feel the stone's protection helping you stay calm and collected.

When the confrontation comes, practice becoming keenly aware and attentive while conversing. Set your emotions aside so that you can problem-solve and see things with greater accuracy.

Bring to mind words of association in your mind that describe interacting with the other party, such as "angry, upset," followed by "breathe, consider" and "confirm, cool down." Practice mindfully responding rather than quickly reacting; this energy will help keep the situation calm.

Quickly and continuously allow your mind to shift between the conversation and the awareness of your necklace and your shield; this reinforces the magick in the moment. While you do this, make sure you don't lose track of the conversation.

Ensure the other person knows that you've heard them and are considering their viewpoints and feelings by briefly summarizing what they've expressed; however, do this in a sympathetic, attentive manner that is not condescending or dismissive. Additionally, remember that you don't need to solve everything immediately in the moment.

If the person you're talking to gets worked up, practice deescalation: Disallow the scenario to become worse, more heated, more argumentative. If needed, remove the trigger in order to do so, even if you yourself are the other person's trigger in the moment. It may go without saying, but if you experience recurring conflict with another person in the form of being demeaned, degraded, or gaslit, separate yourself permanently; your sanity and self-worth are more important than striving for resolution when the other party is not open to it.

Mending Disagreements

If you have experienced an unusual or increasing amount of quarrels, disputes, and disagreements with another person or in the workplace, consider this amulet to encourage gentleness, resolution, and kind communication.

Procure two fresh pieces of all-natural fabric along with a needle and thread. You'll be stitching these two pieces together to create a pouch. Use your intuition to determine the colors and the size of the pouch you'll be creating. On one piece of fabric, draw your name or a sigil or symbol that represents you. On the other, draw the same to represent the person or persons with whom you've had quarrels. These words or drawings can either face inward toward the ingredients or outward depending on what is best for your situation.

Along with a piece of rose quartz and/or selenite (both are said to aid in reconciliation), include any combination of the following herbs in the pouch, all believed by one culture or another to encourage peaceful communication and heal disagreements: valerian, catnip, dandelion, High John the Conqueror root, mugwort, damiana, cinquefoil, rowan, myrrh, broom, and pennyroyal. For additional suggestions, see "Quarrels, to mend" in the correspondences section.

After blending the ingredients, add them to the pouch and stitch it closed while repeating the words:

Mending all quarrels,
All quarrels amend.

Think about each herb you included in the spell, asking them in your own words to "come alive" and help heal disagreements between you and the other party.

You may choose to carry the pouch with you regularly. Otherwise, tuck it somewhere secretly where the disagreements have occurred or where you and the other party frequent together.

Blinding Light: A Cursing Alternative

I don't offer any spells for cursing or hexing in this book because I don't want to be karmically responsible for someone misusing the magickal arts and I believe in the vast majority of cases (but not all!), cursing another person is spiritually immature. Our actions have consequences. The Sanskrit word *karma* simply translates to "action" or "deed."[15]

The spell offered here is an alternative to cursing and is one designed for the greater good. Although it can be seen as a type of defensive magick, this working allows the universe to do the sorting. Consider it a karmic push; a blessing in disguise.

"Enlightening" magick such as this will not harm a person if they are pure in thought and deed. If they are not, however, the result of such a light-blast can synchronistically *rearrange a person's reality* in a manner that *appears* like a curse, but in actuality is a process of karmic sorting that is designed to aid the individual in waking up to the harm they are causing and hopefully change their ways as a result. This magick offers the individual another path, one of compassion and wisdom should they be capable of fostering such qualities. If they choose to continue behavior that directly harms others, however, they will reap the consequences in an expedited manner.

Naturally, if you or someone else is in danger from another person, contact proper authorities, protect yourself and others, and take all the real-world action needed for safety.

Get the person's photo or something connected to them, ideally an object that carries their energy signature. If this is not possible, write their full name on a piece of paper.

Anoint a piece of the stone malachite (used for revealing what is hidden) with essential oils of patchouli and vetiver (for influencing change on someone). Place this on the person's image or item representing them and light a black candle on the left side and a white candle on the right. These candles act as pillars of aware-

15. Grimes, "Karma," 160–62.

ness and carry an esoteric significance not only of balance but of invoking the Pillars of Severity and Mercy found in esoteric Qabalah and related systems.

Sprinkle the herbs eyebright and vervain ideally blended with small chips of tiger's eye. As you do so, envision the person surrounded by cosmic light. Draw this light downward from the cosmos and forcefully cast and project it into the photo or object before you. The easiest way to do this may be raising your left hand upward to invoke the light and pointing a wand or athame in your right hand at the photo or object to precisely command and conduct the vibrational intensity. Conduct this energy while you visualize. Get wide-eyed and intense as you push that white light into every crevice of their being! This light grows and glows and permeates every level of the individual—there is nowhere it doesn't illuminate. Breathe deeply and strongly, seeing divine light entering every pore of their body and layer of their aura. Focus particularly on the light entering and illuminating their brow chakra (*ajna*) and heart chakra (*anahata*), linking their awareness to compassion.

Strongly declare the following after conducting the final blast of light:

[Person's name]*: to the light you must abide,*
With karma returning from every side.
Blinding light and binding light,
You're hereby sanctioned to do what's right.
Kindness and goodness are all that's allowed,
Wisen up, enlighten up, now, now, now!
The errors of your ways you now will see,
As I will, so mote it be!

Disarming & Abolishing Someone Vitriolic

Some people engage in self-serving, malicious behavior that's intentionally damaging toward others. If you feel as though someone in your life is regularly doing such a thing, consider performing this "fuck around and find out" spell but don't use it lightly—carefully consider whether resolution is an option *and* you actually have the full story. If you believe the individual is truly malicious after careful analysis and you need to cut them out of your life, take real-world steps to do this (even legal measures if relevant) alongside performing this spell.

If you're firmly resolute in returning toxic energies and banishing someone from your life, this is a method of doing so in conjunction with proper action in the physical world. If this spell seems too harsh or you sense it could in any way further entangle karmic formations between you and the other person, opt for a different spell from the pages that follow or create a traditional witch bottle (see page 86).

To banish a bitter, vitriolic, unwanted person from your life, write the person's full name (and any nicknames) *backward* on a slip of parchment paper cut to size to fit within your designated glass jar filled with vinegar. The best is called Four Thieves, a popular component in Hoodoo magick, but apple cider or white vinegar are perfectly acceptable.

After writing their name, roll the paper away from your body, stating this or something similar:

[Person's name], *all malice, all harm, all vitriol,*
Now return to you for sorting out. Blessed be and begone!

Tape or tie the roll of paper shut, run it through the flame of a candle (ideally black), and drop it in your jar.

You may also wish to add a rusty nail or coffin nail (another Hoodoo ingredient!) to seal the spell along with a small piece of tiger's eye stone and the herb eyebright to add the intention of opening the eyes. Additionally, garlic, nettles, clove, and poplar buds (balm of Gilead) are useful for banishing someone's influence, and the herbs agrimony and hydrangea are the most renowned for reversing and returning energies to sender. Add the components you wish and personalize the spell to suit your unique situation.

Store this jar in a dark place. When the person is sufficiently out of your life, drain the vinegar down the toilet and toss the remaining contents into the trash with the jar unsealed to release the spell.

The Good Ol' Freezer Spell

Is someone causing trouble and needs to be stopped in their tracks? A classic spell such as this can be helpful, though make sure you feel ethical alignment with performing this type of casting; remember that the wisest methods of shadow magick are designed for the greater good.

As always, if another person poses a physical threat to you, take proper steps to fully banish them from your life and contact proper authorities for assistance.

Procure either the essence of the individual (see the Shadow Reflection on page 83) or simply write their name on a piece of paper. This paper should ideally be parchment, and bonus points for writing the name in bat's blood ink, sold in numerous metaphysical shops (it does not contain any actual blood).

Place the essence or name of the person inside a tight-sealing plastic bag along with a small piece of obsidian. Fill the bag ¾ full with fresh water and seal it tightly. For an added boost, add a splash of stagnant water (see page 172) and/or a large scoop of fresh mud or clay.

Before placing the bag in the back of your freezer, firmly declare the following:

Your wicked influence in my life freezes up,
Stopped in your tracks, no more running amok.
Harmful actions have no room to grow,
By the Powers That Be, this magick I sow.

When you wish to release the spell, melt the ice down the drain or at the base of a tree.

Binding with Sweetness

If someone has been increasingly rude or disrespectful as of late, and you realize that it's not their true nature, try this spell to help sweeten them up and soften their heart.

Inside a glass jar, place either a small poppet representing the person you're working on or simply write their name on a folded sheet of paper. On the jar's lid, or elsewhere in or on the bottle, depending on your intuition, draw the symbol shown here.

Focus intently on the other person's character and actions. Whisper these things into the jar, stating everything about them you've noticed changing, and why you are wanting them to sweeten up immediately.

Drizzle honey into the jar to fully cover the poppet or paper. Finish by including a piece of rose quartz or a handful of rose quartz chips into the jar so it binds to the honey.

Once again, whisper to the individual in question as you explain why you wish for sweetness and kindness to replace their misaligned actions. Tell them why they deserve sweetness and kindness as well as why it's best to treat others in life with a gentle approach.

Once the person has sweetened up and is back to themselves again, unscrew the jar and toss the spell in the trash to be land-filled and released.

Powering Through Shadow

Everyone gets into an emotional slump sometimes, and this spell is designed to help someone who you know is in need. If you are the one experiencing the slump, modify the spell for your purposes accordingly.

If you or someone you know is experiencing an emotional slump, downturn, or energetic blockage and you've done all you can, consider this spell to help inspire action.

Buy a fresh, locally-made, loaf of unsliced bread (or bake one yourself)! Using a serrated knife, carefully cut the loaf into the shape of a large heart. Place this on a plate on your altar or somewhere others won't get into it.

Write the person's name on a small piece of paper and place it on the bread. The stones agate, sunstone, and jasper are all used for inspiring action. Place one or all of these stones atop of paper atop of the bread.

Once situated, light a yellow candle for invigoration and hope. Soften your gaze and hold your hands above the bread. Envision the person smiling and radiant, surrounded in a peaceful glow of healing blue and invigorating yellow.

Speak the following thirteen times:

Facing the shadow can draw us within,
Pull out, pull through; true healing now begins.

The next day, make a cup of coffee and take it with the bread to a natural location. Rip off one piece of bread at a time, dip it in the coffee, and toss it into the wilderness. As you do so, say a prayer for the person each time you dip the bread.

Bow and give thanks to Mother Nature, knowing that you've assisted in the process of powering through a dark tide.

Ambient Energy Feeding

If your energy levels are feeling depleted, one simple and ethical way to absorb others' energy is by ambient or surface feeding. Because this involves taking energy produced by fellow humans, this is particularly relevant for individuals who, often due to trauma, only feel balanced after they've absorbed other people's vital life force (prana or chi/qi), a behavior known as psychic vampirism.

Left uncontrolled, psyvamping can harmfully deplete unwilling peoples' energy and is indeed quite violating. If controlled and approached morally and mindfully, psychic vampirism can be a benevolent practice for those who need it. Please see Michelle Belanger's book in the bibliography for an in-depth study into ethical psychic vampirism.

Go somewhere that energy is produced but not directed for a particular purpose, such as a club's dance floor or overlooking a cityscape. Do *not* draw energy from any person directly but from the overarching amalgamation of energy the people there are passively producing. Psychically perceive the energy above the crowd or city; this energy will eventually dissipate if left undirected, which is why it's available for the taking without causing harm.

Don't take from energy generated from, say, a powwow, an ecstatic dance ceremony, or a political protest, because these energies are being intentionally directed or conducted toward a particular purpose or goal.

The process is simple: dim your vision and secretly inhale slowly and deeply through your mouth as you perceive the ambient energy entering your body and personal sphere. Once complete, send prayers of gratitude to the area that gifted you a boost of vital life-force.

Going Unseen

If you must be in public but would rather go unnoticed for some reason, invisibility spells can be quite helpful. This spell and others of the sort can aid a person in altering their vibrational frequency to a place of becoming largely unnoticed, or only seen on others' periphery. However, do not utilize this sort of magick of you are driving or otherwise need to engage with others for reasons of safety.

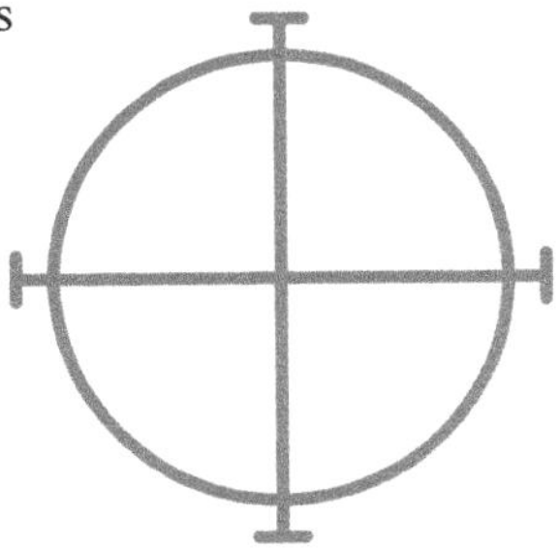

On both sides of a drawstring muslin sachet, draw the symbol shown here.

Inside the bag, combine any of these herbs, all historically alleged to aid in public invisibility: hazel, mistletoe, aconite, poppy, heliotrope, chicory, and most especially any type of fern. You could also add a small bloodstone. Spray or sprinkle your body with witch hazel astringent after completing the bag and before going in public.

Holding your completed sachet, state the following:

My body invisible, in public unseen,
I am aware and my senses are keen.

Carry the bag on person when you wish to go unnoticed in public, and visualize yourself surrounded on all four sides (left, right, behind, and in front) with the same symbol you drew upon the bag. Try not to make eye contact with others unless necessary, and don't dress in a manner that could attract unwanted attention.

Keep the sachet wrapped in black fabric when not in use, and remember to visualize the surrounding symbols dissipating once you wish to be noticed again.

Emergency Vehicle Light-Blast

If an emergency vehicle passes you by, especially an ambulance, it's simple to deduce that someone's experiencing some shit. That is to say, someone is experiencing challenges of shadow and could use a boost of support not only by way of medical help but your own thoughtful energetic work as well.

Energy work can be an act of instant magick; we don't have to ritually prepare, ground our energy, or enter a state of meditation for every act of sending intention. Life itself is an act of sending intention. Instant magick such as this can go a long way and can inspire others to do the same.

When you visibly or audibly become aware of a passing emergency vehicle, raise your right hand and swirl it clockwise, envisioning universal light entering your hand. Quickly hurl this energy in the direction of the vehicle as you say a silent prayer that the energy assist whomever the vehicle is destined toward.

This is a very fast process and will become second nature with practice. Just be sure to invoke cosmic light rather than taking from your own personal energy.

Recovering from Cult Ideology

We all deserve freedom of body and mind. Brainwashing is an insidious process that takes a long time to personally recover from, not to mention the challenging social implications of separating oneself from suffocating systems. It's natural to feel compassion toward the group or dynamic you're leaving, even some level of hesitation, but the fact of the matter is that you've realized it's not for you, and your life is better without its influence.

Whether you're in the process of recovering from actual cult involvement, from cult-like organized religion or politics, from a family dynamic that echoes this behavior, or from any social unit wherein members have extremist ideologies, this moon-to-moon spell may be of assistance. Naturally and depending on the severity of your situation, new community bonds and professional therapeutic help is tremendously advised.

I recommend researching stories, videos, and documentaries from individuals who have survived and escaped cult-like organizations and families; their cases may be triggering but could prove to be inspirational, even if your case is not as extreme as the ones you're researching. Similar stories provide similar energy, and we need both awareness and empathy to thoroughly recover *and* to invoke self-forgiveness.

Plan your spell from one full moon to the next. Think about the intricacies of the situation you've escaped from or are in the process of separating from. Each night from the full moon to new moon, take a fresh piece of paper and write negative beliefs, behaviors, and ideologies associated with the organization or dynamic you're leaving behind. It's okay if some things repeat each session.

After you've written everything you wish, look at the paper and state:

Former restraints,
I set you free,
Harm that was put on me,
You now must flee!

Spit on the paper, sprinkle cloves on top, crumple it up, and throw it in the trash.

To counter this energy, from the new moon to the full moon, write something positive and affirming on a fresh piece of paper each day. These should be statements about your positive attributes, your own actual heartfelt beliefs, and affirmations about the new world you're creating for yourself. After writing and reflecting on each page daily, kiss the paper and keep the pages hidden throughout the lunar cycle; don't toss them out.

On the full moon, burn each page outside with a smile. Declare:

I am me, I am free,
Safe and unbound,
So shall it be.

Remote Help for Those in Crisis

This is a tough one. Sometimes thoughts and prayers for people and animals in crisis just aren't enough. Financial donations, blood donations, petition signings, contacting politicians, and active on-the-ground volunteer work are *incredibly* important, yet sometimes all we have left to give is our energy. We are magickal folk and we *can* energetically help in some small way. In fact, I would say it's our duty.

Whether a war zone, an area hit by a natural disaster, political criminality, or another area afflicted with suffering, we can lend a bit of magick in addition to other means of assistance to those we don't know personally but whom we know are in pain.

After researching the experiences of those whom you wish to gift energetic assistance, decide the steps. Perhaps you have a proclivity of working with spirits and are thus called to help guide those who have crossed over or are in the process of dying. Maybe you're aligned with Reiki or energetic work, feeling most inclined to use your skills to tap into and assist those in crisis from a platform of energetic offering. Perhaps you're especially drawn to the purity of animals and children and wish to offer ritualistic work to help ease pain and panic. And if you don't know your specialty, that's fine! We must work with what we have and what we know.

This entry is not one specific spell but a call to action for you, beloved reader, to value the potency of your unique skills. In addition to whatever work we can do on the earthly plane, our energetic assistance can go a long way. We can't solve all the world's problems, we can certainly choose not to add to them.

When formulating your own spells and magickal work focused on the relief of suffering, consider somehow including flowers and floral essential oils as well as powerful healing stones such as amethyst and rose quartz. Consider the color of candles, such as brown for the animal realm, black for releasing pain, or white for general healing.

Activate the knowledge you have as you perform further metaphysical research with the goal of poignantly projecting energy to the best of your ability; the more specifically focused and directed, the better. We are all connected by an invisible web of life, and every intention is of value: *It all helps*. It's our duty to work both with our shadows and the shadows around us in order to help make the world a better place.

Enchanting Letters of Sociopolitical Action

I'm a big fan of signing online petitions and sending letters. I especially like sending postcards to individuals in corporate or political positions who need a blast of insight to enter their consciousness. Postcards are more likely to be read than sealed letters and are more personal than online petitions. In addition, there's no need for a return address unless you want to make yourself known as a constituent.

However and to whomever you are drawn to share thoughts and feelings with, include the willow tree. Whether it's white willow bark from an herbalist shop or a lovingly harvested branch from a tree, willow is renowned to help in matters of communication and in helping to release any type of pain.

Keep willow near you when creating letters or signing petitions for sociopolitical change. Draw the symbol for the planet Mercury (see symbol on page 122) either under the postage stamp or traced with your finger right before pressing the "send" button on an email or online petition. Communicate your intentions by speaking directly into the paper, phone, or computer.

For an added boost, send the message around the time Mercury goes direct (exits retrograde) or when the Sun or Moon are in zodiac signs ruled by Mercury (Virgo and Gemini). Follow up by energetically sending energy to the person or situation, and encourage others to see what's happening and make their voices heard.

For Gods & Country

If you feel as though your country's political climate is threatening your wellbeing or the wellbeing of others, a little magick can help in addition to on-the-ground work such as financial donations, volunteering, letter-writing, donating blood, educating people, directly assisting those in need, and so on. Whatever the case and even if it isn't focused on a specific incident or occurrence, magickal assistance for a nation and its residents is an act of progressive patriotism.

On your altar or in a sacred space, light candles that represent the colors of your country's flag (or your state, province, or territory). For example, if you live in Brazil, you'll light a yellow candle, a green candle, and a blue candle. Burn dragon's blood resin or an overwhelmingly spicy incense for added potency.

This spell can be modified to help individuals known or unknown in countries other than your own; simply change the candle colors and some of the wording.

With candles and incense burning ideally on a new moon or full moon, situate yourself in meditation and bring up a map of your country, either on paper or a virtual format, and take in the geographic landscape. Think about your knowledge and relation to the country. Along with speaking specific prayers and intentions you may have, declare the following multiple times while focusing on the area:

Om shanti, shanti, shanti
Divine peace prevail!
Protect myself and all who dwell in [name of area].
Divine peace prevail!
Om shanti, shanti, shanti!

Section III

Nature's Shadow Spells

Shadow Reflection: The Virtual Planetarium

We need to be prepared for life's twists and turns, which is why it's wise to keep a magickal arsenal of various herbal mixtures, essential oil blends, and spellcrafting components for any need that may arise.

If you're a fan of astrology or astronomy, check out apps for tablets and smartphones. A number of them are used for planet identification and show users where a planet, galaxy, or constellation is situated. All you have to do is hold up the screen to the sky (or anywhere, really) to view our surrounding cosmic bodies. Many of these apps are free or inexpensive one-time purchases.

If working magick or meditation in conjunction with zodiacal or planetary energy, you can focus on the direction of the planet or constellation to forge a link between you and the cosmos. This "situationship" allows you to draw energy from the physical direction of a cosmic body at any given time, boosting your magickal work with ease.

Shadow Reflection: Toxic Herbcraft

Part of Witchcraft's history includes the usage of poisonous herbs for magickal purposes. The most well-known of these are the Solanaceae family, the nightshades. From usage in banishing poppets to hallucinogenic ointments, toxic herbs have long been revered by Witchy workers of shadow.

The modern practitioner must be mindful when approaching any such plants. Please exercise great caution when using poisonous herbs in any manner, even when touching them or breathing next to them. Never take toxic herbs internally—not even a microdose! With proper research, mindfulness, and focus, we can powerfully integrate toxic herbs in shadow spellwork when the need arises.

CHAPTER 7

Nocturnal Tides & Workings

We shadow workers love to perform our magick, meditations, and contemplations under a gorgeous, mysterious, and shimmery cloak of night. While nighttime isn't required for all workings of shadow, it's certainly an ideal time to weave our heart's desires and glimpse into worlds otherwise unseen.

This chapter begins with a shadow worker's dedication and quickly gets into explorations of the lunar tides. The moon plays a major role in shadow magick and indeed magick in general because of its ever-shifting influence and reliably cyclical presence.

Similarly to the power of the dark and waning moon, the season of autumn and the time of dusk offer shadow workers a beautiful liminality to hone our intentions and reflections. Even occurrences like overcast weather draw our energies inward, potentially aiding processes of self-reflection and emotional transformation.

Nature's shadow is manifold, and the entries in this chapter directly pertain to the comforting and transformative aspects of Mother Nature's shadow. Nature is us and we are her.

A Nocturnal Dedication

On an evening that feels correct—when the stars are aligned as you prefer and when your mind is calm, go outside to a private spot in nature. Draw or wear a crescent moon or triple moon (see symbol) somewhere on your body and declare the following three times:

By nature's glory and the wonder of life,
I dedicate myself as a weaver of shadow and light.
Before the mighty forces of the natural world,
I, [your name], on this evening dark and calm,
Declare my path as a shadow worker for the greater good.
Protect me on this nocturnal path,
By the ebbing tides and my sacred guides,
May I be safe and aware through my life and my work.
Shadow of mine, shadow of others, shadows of the world around,
I dedicate my life to service, to healing, and to the hidden mysteries.
And so it is.

Invocation of the Dark Moon

The dark moon is considered the day before, after, and of the new moon. The two terms are often used interchangeably, similar to how the full moon is considered to have three days surrounding its apex. The dark moon is a time of rebirth and renewal (especially internally), making it ideal for working in this declaration into a greater ritual that includes spellcraft aimed at new beginnings particularly relevant to your life.

This procedure can be a successful addition to or substitute for casting a dark moon circle, and is designed to invoke the dark moon's power of renewal.

Outside and cloaked in a secret place, face the directions one by one, beginning with the east and ending with the north. After saying the following words, proceed with any additional spellcasting or ritualism you've planned:

(East) By the air that fuels my intention,
(South) By the fire that ignites my will,
(West) By the water that nourishes life,
(North) And by the earth that guides my path,
Above and below, within and without,
Guides, gods, and guardians hear my prayers.
My magick comes to life this sacred night.
Dark moon powers I invoke!
Hail and welcome.

Bridging the New & Full Moon

Inspired by author Kate Freuler's incredible book *Of Blood & Bones: Working with Shadow Magick & the Dark Moon*, the concept of capturing your breath in an empty glass jar is a brilliant procedure to incorporate in a wide variety of spellcraft.[16]

16. Kate Freuler, *Of Blood & Bones: Working with Shadow Magick & the Dark Moon* (Llewellyn Publications, 2021), 20.

You can capture your breath in a jar when performing spellcraft that relies on timing. To bridge magickal energy between the full moon and new (dark) moon, you can fill a jar with your breath and open it during the upcoming lunar phase. This is a process of capturing and releasing your personal magickal intention.

Breathe slowly and deeply into a fresh, empty, tight-sealing glass jar upon completing your ritualistic lunar work. You may wish to incorporate herbs, stones, and other components specific to your working, especially (or exclusively) a moonstone.

When the moon has gone through a half-cycle, open the jar to release the initial energy, thereby sealing the spell from either full moon to new moon or new to full.

Releasing Blockages During an Eclipse

Whether a lunar or solar eclipse, and whether full or partial, many cultures throughout time emphasize that this is not a time for performing manifestation work. An eclipse is a peak of liminality (see the following spell for more about liminality), and before scientific advancements, eclipses were considered ominous, surreal, and heavily superstitious occurrences; a "don't mess with the gods while they're doing their thing" sort of vibe!

When a lunar or solar eclipse occurs, it is astronomically called a "syzygy," the alignment of three celestial bodies positioned in a straight line. Instead of focusing on manifestation at these times, consider the apex or interplay of energy between the signs during a lunar or solar eclipse. That is, *solar* eclipses are always new moons, meaning that the moon and sun are in the *same* signs, whereas *lunar* eclipses are always full moons, so the moon and sun are in *opposing* signs according to the Western tropical zodiac (common astrology).

Think of a blockage-releasing meditation and simple candle burning ritual you can do at the exact time of a lunar or solar eclipse. First, research the zodiac sign or signs exalted during the occurrence, and properly research astrological advice to determine where you may blocked in any particular area.

For example, if a lunar eclipse occurs while the opposing signs Leo and Aquarius have an interplay (the Sun is in one and the Moon in another), I may bring to mind creative or expressively blockages specifically and create a meditation around it.

You may wish to incorporate symbols associated with breaking through blockages, such as the symbol on page 54. These could be drawn on paper to be burned, inscribed on candles, drawn on a charm bag, or represented however you wish.

When using any type of eclipse to remove any type of blockage, state the following three times (the number three representing each planetary body) while your intention candle burns:

Mighty eclipse, cosmic forces shifting above,
Release my blockages; I set this into motion!
By the power of this eclipse, I relinquish these obstructions:
[state blockages associated with the eclipse's energy].
Here and now, I move past these, far and beyond,
I open myself to newness as the old falls away.
Here and now, through space and time, mighty Earth, Moon, and Sun,
Aligned, shifting, morphing, I dance with you in reverence.

Harnessing Eclipse Season Liminality

While an eclipse is itself an event of liminality, another eclipse-based liminal time exists during the couple of weeks between two eclipses. Eclipses occur in pairs, a solar following a lunar or vice-versa, due to the three bodies being in such close alignment from Earth's perspective. Many call this 'tween time "eclipse season."

The idea of liminal spaces is a fascinating subject worthy of research! Liminal time or space occurs between one thing and another. Also called a threshold, liminality can feel disorienting or surreal. Naturally occurring liminalities include eclipses, dawn, dusk, midnight, autumn, sleeping, gestation, birth, and death. We experience ritual liminality when standing between the worlds in a magickal or ecstatic ritual. Rites of passage of all varieties can also be considered liminal rituals.

For the purpose of eclipse season, make plans for that roughly two-week period between eclipses. Research the zodiac signs that will be influenced and influenced by the Moon and Sun to determine what kind of work you'd like to perform. Keep in mind that it's commonly stated that magick aimed at *manifestation* is widely advised against during eclipses and eclipse season. Instead, think about how your energy can merge and shift with powers greater than your own. During eclipse season, we are along for the zodiacal and planetary ride, so that time is better spent focused on gestating intention rather than projecting it.

Each day, add to a spell that feels appropriate for the liminal time. You may choose to add one herb, stone, slip of paper, or a different component to a charm bag each day throughout that period, or perhaps integrate a few lines of a poem or new brushstrokes to a piece of art. Allow creativity and magick to merge. Every day (or night) as you reinforce your personally creative work, state the following:

Dawn to dusk, eclipse to eclipse,
I come before the universe as a witness.
This liminal time I harness and respect,
This work I perform has lasting effects.
By shifting powers of space and time,
This magick is united with the Divine.

Shifting at Dusk

You may have noticed that something special happens at the liminal times of dawn and dusk. These shifts are biochemical and physiological, of course, but just like countless things concerning nature and esoterica, our minds and emotions also shift at these times. Some may notice the effect more palpably than others.

While dawn awakens the senses in early risers, dusk holds a special place for those more nocturnal. Diurnal people can absolutely work shadow magick—doing so is one's birthright—but those of us more attuned to nighttime energy have a special penchant for dusk's pleasant threshold.

Whatever your body's rhythm, if you have recently been performing quite a bit of shadow work, I advise regularly honoring the poignancy of dusk.

Go outside at the exact time of sunset and face west, the direction of the setting sun, of release, of shifting frequencies.

Assume a ritual posture if you wish, even simply raising one arm in adoration. For occult reasons far too long to explain here, the ideal western quadrant ritual posture is to have feet together, forming an outward V with heels touching, while your fingers form an open downward triangle at the belly (thumbs touching and pointer fingers touching).

State the following before taking a bow, and feel free to present offerings and spells to the setting sun as you see fit:

Shifting dusk and shadow rising, my energy draws within.
By the downgoing of the sun, when one thing ends another begins.
By the primordial waters of creation,
Please empower my transformations!
So mote it be.

Releasing with Autumn

Autumn is a special time of year for darkly-inclined magickal folks. Similarly to how energy shifts every day at dusk, autumn can be looked at as the year's annual dusk. Days grow shorter and nights grow longer, offering an ideal time to release thoughts, feelings, emotions, experiences, hindrances, and challenges that no longer serve to make one's life better.

This ongoing shadow spell can be performed on its own *or* in addition to the sabbat-to-sabbat spell for the Autumn Equinox on page 188.

On the Autumnal Equinox, place a large jar or container on your altar or somewhere special. Inside it, place a small amount of herbs for banishing and releasing (see correspondences). On that evening and every evening between then and Samhain (Halloween), add a small slip of paper that either states or represents one thing you intend to banish or release. If some end up repeating, that's okay. Let creativity take hold as you decide during the course of each day, what you'd like to lay to rest this season.

Ceremonially burn all these papers together with the herbs in a fire either on October 31 or "astrological Samhain," on or around November 6.

Stillness with Gloomy Weather

Dark, overcast, drizzly, or otherwise gloomy weather holds a special place in the hearts of those prone to introspection and shadow work. Although depressing for some, we can take advantage of dreary days by slowing down and recalibrating our thoughts.

Situate yourself outside to fully observe and absorb the environment. Light a stick of your favorite incense as an offering, ensuring that it will burn down in a safe spot.

Bring attention to your breath. Breathe in through the nose and out through the mouth. Practice fourfold "box breathing" for a few minutes: Inhale slowly to the count of four, hold the breath deeply (down to the diaphragm) to the count of four, exhale to the count of four, hold (with no breath in the lungs) to the count of four, and repeat.

Continue to meditate as long as you need, visualizing your energy merging with the environment. When ready, state the following four times:

Shadow within, shadow without,
My body is calm, my mind is chilled out.

Deeply Grounding Oneself

If you've been feeling especially stressed out lately, deeply invoke the element earth to help balance overactive thoughts (air), emotional overwhelm (water), and generalized anxiety (fire).

Make a plan to cover your body in mud under cloak of night. This deep "earthing" activity is most definitely out-of-the-norm but can be greatly beneficial. Temporarily shifting out of one's ordinary paradigm aids in altering consciousness and generating a mystical state of mind.

You may dig your own soil and mix it with water, purchase organic topsoil and do the same, or even perform the activity with clay. If using clay, I suggest purchasing powdered bentonite clay from an herbal supplier; when mixed with water, this clay is known to be purifying internally and externally, physically and metaphysically.

After covering your entire body with mud, clay, or a mixture of the two, visualize Mother Earth's calming, healing energy entering the bottoms of your feet, filling your entire being. With each exhale, visualize stress exiting your body and sticking to the mud. If you wish, use your fingers to draw stars and spirals on your muddy body.

When you shower off, visualize the stress washing away and the essence of deep grounding radiating from your squeaky-clean epidermis.

After a good night's sleep, you should wake up feeling refreshed and ready to take on whatever life has to offer.

A Witching Hour Masquerade

The folkloric term "Witching hour" has a number of interpretations as a liminal time of spiritual potency. Some say it's midnight. Others cite 3:00 a.m. Some say it encompasses the hours between midnight and 3:00 a.m. Still others cite 3:33 specifically, while some cite the peak of night, which would be the midpoint between sunset and sunrise; if sunset is at 8:00 p.m. and sunrise is at 6:45 a.m., for example, the peak of the night and therefore the Witching hour would be at 2:15 a.m.

After determining your own definition of the Witching hour, research various manners of crafting masks or crowns from natural materials. Twigs, leaves, pressed flowers, herbs, grasses, and grains are but a few examples of materials that can be woven, glued, tied, wrapped, or otherwise affixed to create your own unique crown or mask exclusively for shadow work.

When the Witching hour you've decided on arrives and while in a sacred space, place the piece on your body while stating its mystical intention in your own words. Dedicate the piece to shadow work and enchant it through the elements however you see fit. Each time you put it on, envision yourself shifting to an altered state of consciousness that will hopefully help you more easily operate in and occupy a mystical space between the worlds.

Don your piece before performing magickal work appropriate to your life's current situation, and reenchant the piece every dark moon, ideally at the Witching hour.

CHAPTER 8
Shadowcraft Components

Because shadow work is an ongoing process, the wise practitioner remains prepped and equipped with a variety of tools pertinent to our Craft.

This chapter consists of shadow-based tools and ingredients that are best kept on the shelf (or altar) for when the need arises. Many of these can be jarred and are quite long-lasting, like graveyard dirt, black salt, and herbal mixtures used for banishing. Some of these components are naturally occurring, while others take a bit of effort to create or procure.

A number of waters are also explored in this chapter, including suggested metaphysical uses of stormwater, stagnant water, and Mars water.

The enchantment of nocturnal jewelry and occult books are mentioned here because these are a shadow worker's extension of both nature *and* one's inner nature. Bones and animal bits are examined with suggestions on how to mindfully obtain and use them in shadow magick.

Although this is a brief list of entries in the scope of shadow-based ritual tools, I feel they are some of the most important to be aware of and to keep handy for magickal work of the darker but not necessarily harmful variety.

A Shadow Work Prep Potion

Shadow work is incredibly versatile and interpretive. The style has many branches and approaches—and also roots.

The roots of plants and trees can be considered the underground connectors that link to the Underworld and chthonic realms. Roots often represent hidden things as well as potency. Seeing as the word "occult" means "concealed or hidden," it's no wonder that the roots of plants and trees have long played a special role in magickal cultures for millennia.

One method of crafting a shadow work potion is to take thirteen roots, the number of lunar cycles in a year, and boil them for thirteen minutes in a cauldron or on the stovetop. While they boil and the timer counts down, speak words of power into the mixture. This is a versatile potion, so it all comes down to how you wish to use it in the future.

Add thirteen ice cubes and allow the mixture to come to room temperature. Strain the roots and dispose of them outside as offerings. Keeping the potion in a jar that you can use during shadow magick of all varieties, from dreamwork to necromancy to past-life regression.

You may choose to asperge (sprinkle) this potion during a shadow working, to anoint your brow, to cleanse ritual and divinatory tools, and so on. Don't use it internally unless every chosen ingredient is safe. Refrigerate and use within one lunar cycle or freeze the concoction for longer usage.

Creating Black Salt

Also called Witch's salt, black salt is used in a wide variety of magickal systems and folk practices. The metaphysical essence of black salt makes use of two protective aspects: the color black and salt as a mineral. Both salt and the color black are used for protection as well as for banishing and releasing.

I must say, black salt helps create a remarkably powerful rampart of protection! It's wise to always have a bit of black salt on hand to assist with certain types of shadow work.

If you'd like to craft your own, the simplest recipe is to acquire rock salt (it is more effective for the aforesaid purposes than sea salt), and a small amount of activated charcoal powder. This powder can be found at herbal and health food stores and is used medically in small amounts to internally aid the body in detoxification or absorption of harmful substances.

Simply blend the two ingredients, ideally powdering them with a mortar and pestle. You may also wish to add the ashes of specific herbs you've burned. If you're using the salt for protection, it's wise to powder some dried eggshells with the black salt or add cascarilla eggshell powder, which is frequently used in Hoodoo and related systems.

As you sprinkle the salt whether along the windowsill, your home's doorway thresholds, or as a component in spellcraft, it's good practice to repeat the words, "Negativity neutralized *now*!"

Crafting Banishing Balls

We need to be prepared for life's twists and turns, which is why it's wise to keep a magickal arsenal of various herbal mixtures, essential oil blends, and spellcrafting components for any need that may arise.

Shadow magick frequently includes work for banishing and releasing. An easy go-to for this purpose are clay banishing balls. These premade balls can be utilized in a variety of ways in spellcraft, such as crumpling them up in handwritten petitions, throwing them on an alchemical fire, dissolving them in water, burying them with prayers of release, leaving them hidden in certain locations, and so on.

Gather and blend a number of herbs used for banishing and releasing (see correspondences), including any herb in the nightshade family. For an added boost of banishing and releasing, incorporate the three S's: snakeskin, sulfur, and salt (or black salt; see the previous spell).

After blending the components, acquire all-natural, fresh sculpting clay. Simply work the ingredients into the clay and form them into half-inch balls. Carve the symbol shown here onto each banishing ball. Allow these to fully dry before storing them in a glass jar.

When it's time to use them in magick, it's ideal to burn dragon's blood resin for added potency and repeat words of power associated with your intention to banish.

Collecting Stagnant Water

A powerful tool to keep in one's magickal toolbox is stagnant water, the most potent being water from a bog, swamp, marsh, or bayou. This powerful spellcraft component is used for releasing stuck, stagnant, toxic energy *or* for slowing someone down who may be working magick against you. (If you're trying to slow down someone's attacks, another option is to make a spell using a jar of mud or clay.) The water can be used in numerous ways; just think about the meaning of stagnation and toxicity and incorporate it in your magick however you see fit.

Do not ingest the water and be careful when using it on your skin (do so only briefly, if ever) because the plethora of bacteria, microorganisms, and parasites that can cause adverse reactions and illness. Suggestions for use include drizzling it atop spells aimed at releasing what is stuck, charging the water with intentions of release before flushing it, and chanting anti-stagnation words of power while putting some on your body immediately before a shower. In the case of the latter, visualize your own stuck energies entering the water right before the shower's new, fresh, and active water rejuvenates and refreshes your personal energy.

Visit a swamp or other location where water accumulates and sits there but is not as clean as a lake or spring. Bottle the water in a tight-sealing glass jar and leave an offering in gratitude before leaving. If animals frequent that location, leave an edible offering they will enjoy. Otherwise, cornmeal, tobacco, or a small crystal will suffice.

As you leave the offering, state something like, "My gratitude extends to all beings in this area; thank you for your blessings."

Enchanting Stormwater

Thunderstorms offer an atmosphere of excitement and empowerment. The electromagnetic surge affects our bodies, minds, and spirits, reminding us of Mother Nature's immense power—and our own.

Storm water is an excellent magickal component to keep on hand, so next time there's a heavy storm in your area, have some buckets on hand to collect the water.

Thunderstorm rain carries invigorating energy and can be bottled for future use in magick that requires an extra boost. To collect and use this unique water is to create a liquid time capsule of sorts.

Once the storm has passed and you've collected all the water you desire, place it in an airtight glass jar along with a quartz crystal and label the bottle for future use. Both the stormwater and the quartz are used for boosting intention and adding power. Adding a splash to bathwater or floor wash goes a long way!

Label the water and go outside after the storm has subsided. Hold the jar high above you while recalling the storm. Imagine the water surging, vibrating, and filled with the storm's mighty power and mysterious energy.

Shake up the bottle while declaring:

A mighty storm has gifted this natural libation,
This water is charged with life and invigoration!

Invigorating Mars Water

Although its use in shadow magick is infrequent, it's a good idea to have Mars water on hand for specific purposes. As a planet, Mars rules the sign Aries (and Scorpio in classical astrology). Aries can be seen as the force of spring; the potency of new life forging through the waning winter's hesitation. Scorpio can be seen as the deepest, darkest depth of emotion, embodying life's passion, mystery, and intensity.

As a magickal component, Mars water can be used in spells to banish anger, to power through obstacles, and to protect a person under psychic attack. Its alternate name, war water, also speaks to its destructive potency to inflict injury and chaos.

If you have stormwater, add some to a jar along with a pinch of black salt (see page 171). Introduce a small volcanic rock to the mix for added potency, or a piece of red coral; the latter is the primary stone of Mars according to Jyotisha (Vedic/Indian/Hindu astrology).

After filling the jar with pure, fresh water, add four large nails. These nails must be made of iron or steel so that they will rust, eventually turning the water into a Martian hue of rusty red. Another option is to procure a steel railroad spike, ideally one that was actually embedded in a railroad track at one time. Label the jar with the symbol for Mars (see symbol on previous page).

Shake up the bottle on a regular basis while vocally repeating the names of the water's three rulerships: Mars, Aries, and Scorpio. Keep it safe and use it wisely!

Exalting Bones as Ritual Tools

In shadow magick, bones can become magickal tools for anything from protection to necromancy to the invocation of ancestral wisdom. The ins and outs of working with bones both animal and human are far too deep to get into here and now, so what follows is a general enchantment.

Gently cradle your bone or bones in front of your altar at midnight, ideally wrapped in a black cloth with a piece of amethyst accompanying. Consider their source—human remains or animal. If animal, think about the species and which qualities the species represents. Consider the particular bone(s) you have: Which part of the body did they come from, and how does this relate to your magickal work and your life at present?

While you envision the bone(s) glowing in every color of the rainbow, as well as black and white, whisper the following to them three times:

Sacred bone(s), I honor your presence.
Physical frame, I offer you a home.
Skeletal remains, I ask for your blessing.
Peaceful friend(s), please aid my work.

Honoring Graveyard Dirt

Similarly to the case of working with bones for shadow magick, a full description of graveyard dirt would be impossible to fit in these pages. However, the main point to consider is the source: From whose grave did you gather the dirt? Or was it gathered from burial grounds in general?

Graveyard dirt, also called grave dust, is used in Hoodoo for numerous spellcasting intentions. If you're unfamiliar with its manifold usage in magickal work, please research it thoroughly before proceeding.

If gathering real dirt from a graveyard or cemetery, offer a dime, some liquor, or a flower in addition to a handful of grains. Only take a small amount of dirt that doesn't leave a visible hole in the ground. And of course, be secretive and selective in this process.

If you'd prefer to make an herbal substitute for grave dust, powder and bottle a combination of the herbs mullein, valerian, and patchouli. The mullein included should be the plant's dried leaf, valerian its dried root, and the patchouli portion its leaves, roots, or a combination. Another powerful option is to combine this powder with actual graveyard dirt.

When you gather the dirt or powder the herbs, state the following four times:

Graveyard dirt, swept and collected,
You're held reverence, safe and protected.
Darkness of earth, secrets of the beyond,
Please aid my magick; make it strong.

Using Hairballs, Owl Pellets & Vomit

When approaching spellcraft, consider sympathetic magick, also called imitative magick, where something represents something else. It's icky, I know, but owl pellets, kitty cat hairballs, and any type of vomit can be used in shadow work for the purposes they embody in the physical world: rejection. These components can be used to combat harmful energies put upon you from others or from life in general.

If you believe you're under psychic attack, have been cursed, or if harassment is at an all-time high, the energy of these occurrences is the same: energetic harm.

Most cat owners know what it's like to discover a hairball; well, better out than in! This putrid object can be dried and saved for magickal use or used immediately in a spell for rejecting energies put upon you.

Unlike owl feathers, owl pellets are legal to purchase in the US, and a handful of magickal supply shops and online retailers offer them. Other retailers offer different animal bits one can use for releasing or banishing magick such as snakeskin, tarantula sheds, and dried poop from wild animals.

As for vomit, a pet's vomit can be collected should they have an upset tummy, though, of course, your own vomit is most effective in focusing energy directed at rejecting harmful energies that have been put upon you personally. I won't get into details about collecting this, but please don't force yourself to puke just for an ingredient!

Ideally during a waning moon cycle, assemble a spell that represents all the energies you believe have been placed upon you to cause harm, confusion, or mishap. This could be in the form of a petition (parchment paper is best), a banishing bag containing herbs for banishing, a witch bottle (see page 86), or something else.

When you add the rejective component to the spell, declare:

Refused, unwanted, entirely rejected!
Negativity put on me becomes deflected.
Harmful energies must hereby flee!
As I will, so shall it be.

Charging Nocturnal Jewelry

Many people wear certain pieces of jewelry or other accessories only at nighttime. Some wear this jewelry only on fancy dinners or a night on the town. For others, specific rings, pendants, necklaces, and other accessories are reserved exclusively for ceremonial and ritualistic use. Whatever your nocturnal usage, it's wise to empower nocturnally dedicated pieces on a regular basis.

Using a sterile lancet or needle, prick the middle finger of your right hand. Mix three drops of blood with an anointing oil of your choice.

As you respectfully anoint each piece of jewelry, state:

Dark as night and bright as will,
These pieces hone my shadow skills.
These sacred charms are borne divine,
And come alive through space and time.

Enchanting a Book of Shadows

At this point in the history of Witchcraft, the definition of a Book of Shadows (BoS) is quite diverse! Emerging from 1950s Gardnerian Wicca, the Book of Shadows was an initiatory coven's central text and was to be copied verbatim by a lineage's oathbound initiates. A great many covens, Gardnerian and otherwise, preserve this powerful recordkeeping practice to this day.

These days, a Book of Shadows can also refer to a person's private mystical journal that documents magickal wisdom, lessons, spells, rituals, charms, correspondences, mythologies, personal reflections, dream interpretations, divination results, and anything else relevant to the writer's spiritual journey. While there are also a great many virtual BoS manuals and printed books for purchase, the enchantment below is designed for your *personally handwritten* magickal book or journal.

This magickal book should be both an extension of the Self and extension of Mother Nature, which is why we will make use of the elemental powers. This is an exceedingly simple elemental enchantment, but this manner of charging items is standard for a reason—it's marvelously effective!

Within a sacred space or cast circle, face each direction as you use a physical element to bless the tome: incense or feathers for air, flame or lava rock for fire, fresh water or saliva for water, and salt or stone for earth.

Once you've entered a focused state of mind, declare at each direction:

(East) By powers of air, I dedicate this book as a record of wisdom!
(South) By powers of fire, I dedicate this book with spiritual inspiration!
(West) By powers of water, I dedicate this book as an evolving work of art!
(North) By powers of earth, I dedicate this book as sacred and safe!
(Above) By powers above, I dedicate this book with cosmic light!
(Below) By powers below, I dedicate this Book of Shadows!

Hug the book close to your heart and use a sterile lancet to anoint the book with your blood, such as a thumbprint on the inner cover, in order to link it to you personally and deeply for life.

Dedicating an Occult Library

We occultists, mystics, and Witchy types are natural bookworms. Virtual eBooks can be fun, but there's something special about printed-and-bound physical tomes.

The word "occult" refers to that which is hidden or shrouded—like the mysteries of the universe, for one! The information and wisdom we seek isn't everyone's cup of tea, but it's all part of the quest to understand ourselves and the nature of this perplexing reality. We are called toward wisdom and understanding, and we choose not to be dissuaded by superstition or cultural norms. We won't settle for placation or toxic theologies because we are inspired to analyze existence and come to our own informed conclusions.

It's a wise idea to empower your personal esoteric library of printed books however great or small it may be. This spell can help you more deeply bond with your books, and you're likely to notice your intuition increase in this regard. For example, you may be searching for information on a specific metaphysical topic and know exactly which book to grab off the shelves. You may feel a magnetic pull from a particular book and synchronistically discover that it provides insight into a current situation in life. Expect the unexpected!

Rosemary is burned for knowledge, wisdom, study, and memory. Decide how you will burn rosemary for the spell: do you have a dried bundle of the herb, or would you prefer to use an incense charcoal? If you wish, additionally burn some frankincense resin. You'll also want to safely extract a few drops of your own blood to burn with the herb, which will help bind your deepest energy to the essence of the books.

When you're prepped in front of your bookshelf or library, take some time to focus on the tomes before you. Contemplate their histories. How did they make way into your hands and into your life? Is your library well-organized or in need of some upkeep? Which are yet to be read, and which do you want to read again? Which were gifts and which did you purchase yourself? Where are their authors now?

After taking deep breaths and feeling a sense of reverence for the books before you, light the herb and/or resin you've accented with blood. As you waft the smoke around every title, declare:

I fumigate this space and honor these sacred texts!
Come alive, beloved books of magick and wisdom!
Speak to me, link with me, and aid in my evolution!
I am your safe-keeper, and on the ethers we are bound!

CHAPTER 9

Sabbat Shadow Magick

The concept of the eight sabbats was solidified in Wicca, the well-known movement of modern European-based Witchcraft begun by Gerald Gardner in the early 1950s. Sabbats occur on the two equinoxes, the two solstices, and the four approximate cross-quarter days, making them both solar and astrological. Sabbats are now widely observed by a variety of Neopagan spiritualities and nature-based practices of Witchcraft.

If workers of shadow magick predominantly align with the moon in their Craft, why would they follow the cycles of the sun and its holidays?! Well, for one, the sun illuminates our beloved moon. Secondly, not every sabbat is bright and shiny!

Naturally beginning with the beautiful dark tide of Samhain, this small chapter dances along the Wheel of the Year with the shadow worker in mind. Truly, at every turn of the Wheel, there's work to be done in both shadow and light.

We can harness both waning and waxing solar energy to assist in our shadow work. This chapter gives a handful of suggestions on how we can align with these seasonal shifts in accordance with our darker proclivities.

Samhain: Dark Arts

At Samhain (Halloween), the final harvest is collected and life's energy begins to wane, making it the ideal time for banishing and releasing. Beautiful, dark, and Witchy, Samhain falls between autumn and winter.

Create a piece of visual art that represents everything you desire to banish from your life. Consider affixing herbs and black salt (see page 171) for the purpose alongside words, symbols, and imagery that entirely embody all the negative stuff you want to remove from your life. For suggestions, see the list of materials used for banishing and releasing in this book's correspondences.

To get the ball rolling on this process, burn your piece of dark art in a Samhain fire while boldly stating your intentions. As each portion of the piece burns, visualize the flame consuming and transforming those hindrances, banishing that shit to become fertilizer for better things and brighter days.

Winter Solstice: Rebirthing

Midwinter is the time of rebirth. This is reflected in Pagan traditions of Yule with the rebirth of the sun, the Oak King, solar deities, and in other traditions as the rebirth of the "son" or saving grace.

In the dead of Solstice night, situate yourself in a secret place outdoors. Cover your body with a veil or blanket, head to the ground as your deep breaths meet the cold earth. Gently begin moving your body and growing taller. Slowly, very slowly, gather more energy; this represents the return of life and light, within and without.

Eventually burst from the veil or blanket, throwing it aside, eyes cast to the quiet sky. Draw cosmic light into your body and declare the return of the sun!

Imbolg: Lights in the Dark

Also called Candlemas, Imbolg (or Imbolc) is an ancient Celtic holiday falling between winter and spring. Naturally, we want to use candlelight in association with shadow work at this time.

Sit in a circle and situate six candles around you; this will form a hexagonal shape. Bring to mind all the shadows you've been dealing with lately, internally and interpersonally. As each troublesome thought arises, use your hands or magickal tool to sweep your body from toe to head, directing each challenging thought into the flame.

Each time you offer a shadow to the flame, say the word "transformed." Envision the light from each flame outshining every point of darkness you offer up.

Spring Equinox: From Darkness into Light

The Sun enters Aries on this day, also called Ostara. This shift secures the promise of new life and provides an excellent time to focus on the alchemization of shadow to light.

To harness this seasonal energy internally, learn the Sanskrit *pavamāna mantra*. This Hindu mantra from the *Upanishads* (part of the holy Vedas) is appropriate for the season; it translates as: "From the unreal to the real; from darkness into light; from death to immortality; peace, peace, peace."

Facing the sun on Ostara, recite the mantra (if you like, look up pronunciation online beforehand):

Asato mā sadgamaya;
tamaso mā jyotirgamaya;
mṛtyormā'mṛtaṃ gamaya;
shanti, shanti, shanti.

Beltane: A Fivefold Kiss

The traditional Wiccan fivefold kiss is a blessing action a high priest or priestess (or one acting as such in ritual) makes, often during initiatory rituals or during the ceremonial Great Rite (a symbolic or actual sexual union).

Because many shadow workers struggle with self-love (often the result of imprints from past traumatic experiences), we can modify the blessing to invoke a bit more self-respect and compassion in our lives. Beltane, landing between spring and summer, is a time of love. This makes a solitary loving blessing all the more appropriate and meaningful.

Wear a rose quartz necklace and stand at your altar skyclad (nude). Sprinkle the herb cinquefoil (five-finger grass) around you. This plant's leaves look like a human hand, a symbol of our capability and capacity, as well as the five virtues of love, money, health, power, and wisdom. You may also wish to sensually masturbate and take a luxurious bath or shower after performing the kiss three times.

Kiss your right hand's forefinger and middle finger together before touching each part of your body and reciting the following after each kiss:

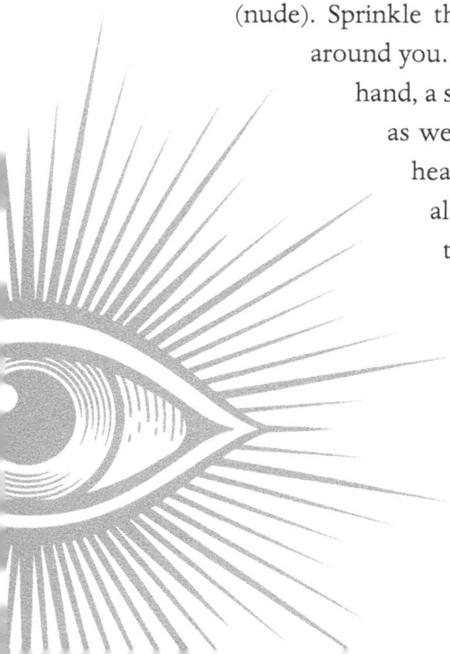

(Feet) Blessed be my feet, that have brought me in these ways.

(Knees) Blessed be my knees, that kneel at the sacred altar.

(Navel) Blessed be my loins, without which we would not be.

(Chest) Blessed be my chest, formed in perfect strength.

(Lips) Blessed be my lips, which shall utter the sacred names.

Summer Solstice: Knot Magick

Also called Midsummer or Litha, the Summer Solstice is the time when the archetypal Holly King begins to take power. This is the longest day of the year; there's so much light—what's a shadow worker to do with all this brightness?! Believe it or not, this day gives us a great opportunity to capture solar light in the form of knot magick.

Calculate the time of the sun's peak; this will be the midway point between sunrise and sunset. For example, sunrise is at 5:30 a.m. and sunset is at 9:00 p.m., the peak of the day would be at 1:15 p.m.

Get a long cord that can be tied thirteen times, and gather thirteen flowers (ideally sunflowers or yellow roses) that can be tied into each knot. Hold the flowers and the cord up to the sun while tying each knot.

This light can be released in the future by simply untying a knot, honoring the flower, and deeply inhaling the captured solar vibration. It's ideal to untie knots later throughout the year's darker tides, when you're feeling particularly solemn, sad, or uninspired.

Lammas: Resting the Shadow

Also called Lughnasadh, the ancient Celtic festival of Lammas falls between summer and autumn. This midway point is an excellent time to begin working with shadowy energies we will continue to work with during the darker parts of the year.

Some traditions of Witchcraft teach a person to "bury, burn, or sink" the components of a spell after performing. Naturally, we need to take ecological considerations into account, as we don't want to be part of the problem!

A great way to utilize natural components at this time of year is to gather and wash a number of rocks, ideally two to five inches in length; not too big, not to small. On each stone, use natural ink to write on the stones. Write words that directly state things in your life that no longer serve you, whether they are emotions, judgments, or external hindrances you've been experiencing in life.

On Lammas night, light a black candle and grasp each stone with tongs, running each one through the flame until each rock is blackened. Now that they're burnt, you can bury each stone in a container of dirt (consider using graveyard dirt for this; see page 176). Finalize by sinking: Dump the mixture of stones and dirt into a flowing river and be sure to offer a handful of grains to the wandering spirits and creatures.

Autumn Equinox: Discarding the Unwanted

The sun enters Libra on the Autumn Equinox, also called Mabon. In conjunction with our preparations for Samhain, we can begin to form either a banishing bag or a piece of dark art to be burned in a Samhain fire (see page 184).

Begin collecting items that represent or embody the things you intend to release or banish. Suggestions include fallen leaves, dead bugs you've discovered, snakeskin, tissues used when crying, black salt (see page 171), cobwebs, written slips of paper, bills for outstanding debts, dead plant leaves, black candle wax, and herbs used for banishing and releasing (see correspondences).

Dedicate either the sachet bag or the canvas at this time; whatever you plan to place on the fire next sabbat. As the sun sets, which itself creates the symbol of Libra (see page 57), hold the item or items to the sunset, and talk to your guides, gods, and guardians. Explain what the item(s) are for and what you aim to achieve during this year's shadow tide. Use the time between now and Samhain to regularly add to the spell in an act of sabbat-to-sabbat shadow magick.

Section IV

Otherworld Shadow Spells

Shadow Reflection: The Seen & Unseen

Our whole reality is an interplay of visible and invisible energy. The thoughts and emotions we have are, themselves, invisible. We are well aware that the physical world is only one slice of multifold reality, and that every level and layer should also be kept in mind.

Some people are more prone to perceive and interact with unseen forces that are conscious or carry a level of sentience—spirit guides, spirit animals, ancestors, guardians, astral entities, gods, goddesses, and deities are but some of these.

The more deeply our spiritual wisdom increases, the easier we can perceive and learn to navigate our own continual relationship with unseen forces.

Sleep and dreaming are, by their very nature, directly connected to the realm of shadow. Just as the sun descends and the moon wanes, our bodies, minds, and spirits must rejuvenate with good, solid, restful sleep.

Shadow Reflection: The Passage of Time

On the other side, the passage of time is not as linear as it appears in this dimension. When working with spirits, guides, deities, ghosts, and other forms of nonphysical consciousness, it's helpful to keep in mind that their perceived experiences are different from our own.

> We are but fractal fractures of infinite spirit temporarily embodying beautiful and often complicated physical frames, the ego and mind included … We must be our own advocates because we're here for a reason and life is already short as-is. Fight for your happiness!

We sometimes hear stories of ghosts lingering for centuries and beloved childhood pets waiting to greet someone once they've shuffled off their mortal coil. We can theorize all we wish—or even research near death experiences or receive our own visions of what's next—but the fact remains that in these bodies, we aren't quite capable of perceiving how things work over there. Still, we must rest assured that they work at their own pace, and that our interactions with the unseen are real, meaningful, and timely.

CHAPTER 10

Interacting with the Unseen

We now shift our focus to shadow work that deals specifically with unseen energy. Naturally, this chapter opens with methods for charging tools of divination. Whenever we divine and in whatever form, we are tapping into unseen energy. That energy can originate internally from the unconscious mind, externally from alternate planes of reality, or come from a combination of the two.

Also covered in this chapter is the banishing and casting away of harmful spirits and accumulated invisible energy that shouldn't be hanging around. We will explore what to do when such harmful influences attempt to take hold. It is our right and responsibility to energetically upkeep not only ourselves but also our environments.

Just the same, it's essential to honor the guides and guardians on the inner planes whose influence (normally under the radar of human consciousness) regularly plays a part in guiding our daily intuition and carrying our magickal intentions.

With enough practice, we can learn to determine and decipher which invisible energies and entities we desire to work with versus which need to be sent away. There is a whole world around us waiting to be perceived!

Enchanting Tools of Divination

Divination itself is a type of shadow work. To divine is to gaze into the unseen or the unknown. Divination helps a person garner insight from that which exists beneath the surface of everyday consciousness.

On a new moon, place all your tools of divination on an altar or table in front of you: all tarot and oracle decks, runes, crystal balls, pendulums, dowsing rods, scrying mirrors, and so on.

Brew a strong cup of mugwort tea and use a sterile lancet to mix in a few drops of your blood, ideally from the ring finger of your right hand. The purpose of the blood is to bind each tool to you. Note that this also means any item enchanted in this manner should not be used by another person.

As you either wash each item in the cooled tea or simply asperge (sprinkle) the tea atop each item, honor each tool individually by holding it to your heart in gratitude for the gift it provides. Throughout the process, repeat the following:

Tools of wisdom, you provide clear insight.
On this darksome night you come alight!

Empowering a Scrying Tool

Scrying is one of the oldest forms of divination, and everyone has a different method of doing so. Although Hollywood shows crystal balls and magick mirrors in an entertaining light, the symbolism received by the diviner isn't usually quite so glamorously prophetic.

Symbols, images, and patterns make themselves known as the practitioner gazes into a dark, enchanted item. These can be interpreted for wisdom, prediction, and Otherworldly communication.

Get your tool for scrying whether it's a crystal ball, a dark bowl filled with water, a large black stone like obsidian, a black mirror designed for this purpose, or something else.

Make a strong infusion of mugwort, either brewing a tea or purchasing a tincture. On a dark moon at midnight, wash your scrying device with this mixture and don't buff the item's surface until the next day. As you wash the tool, say:

Darkened moon, and tool of night,
I imbue you as a link to my unconscious.
Washed with care, and gazed with intent,
May all the visions I perceive be true and wise.

Fire & Brimstone Protection

A very simple spell to rid an area of negative vibes and spirits (or at least jump-start the process) is to use sulfur. Also called brimstone, sulfur is found on the head of most safety matches. The best choice are stick matches in a box whose sides are used to ignite each match.

In each area you wish to chase out stagnant or harmful vibes, strike a match and blow it out after the sulfur has fully burned. Make a plan to burn natural incense of a high vibration after completing the process, the most ideal being frankincense or copal.

Each time you strike a match, firmly declare:

Begone, begone, begone!
All that is harmful must flee!
All that is stagnant must disperse!
Begone, begone, begone!

To add extra potency to this and any other ritual that works strongly with spirit banishing, incorporate a banishing pentagram of earth (see previous page). This should be drawn invisibly with the pointer finger of your dominant hand or an athame quite largely in front of your body, beginning and ending at the bottom left corner of the symbol as pictured. This pentagram can be traced in the air wherever you genuinely feel a harmful presence or need an energetic reset.

A pentagram traced in this manner is believed to repel malevolent terrestrial energy, including negative projections from other people and from spirits. This particular elemental banishing pentagram is also used when facing each of the four directions while performing the Lesser Banishing Ritual of the Pentagram (LBRP), a purifying and archangelic ritual popularized by the Golden Dawn.[17]

17. Donald Michael Kraig, *Modern Magick: Twelve Lessons in the High Magickal Arts* (Llewellyn Publications, 2010), 50.

Hypercleansing a Room

Negative or stagnant energy can sometimes fester in a single area. These energetic swamps can be strongly cleansed with camphor. Used most often in Hindu ceremonies like pujas and homas, camphor blocks can be found in both Indian marketplaces and occult shops. Camphor is also used in Hoodoo and related traditions for purposes of cleansing and purification, where it is believed to invite higher energies in place of lower ones.

Camphor is a resin from the camphor laurel evergreen tree. Its strong fragrance is pure menthol. Don't breathe in too much smoke when burning, and figure out a way to safely handle the burning block. I prefer to use incense tongs and place the block atop a bowl of sand.

Enter the room or space in need of a hypercleansing and ignite the camphor in its dish. Starting from the walls walk around the area widdershins (counterclockwise) in a spiral pattern, each circumambulation becoming smaller and smaller until you spiral into the center.

Place the hot dish on the floor, allowing the camphor to fully burn down. As it does, recite the words mentioned in the previous spell or something similar. Be sure to open doors and windows so the smoke and energy have somewhere to flee!

Spirit-Banishing with Loban

Loban resin is also called gum benzoin, styrax, and storax. The Hindi term *loban* was originally called *lōbanā* in Sanskrit and *lubān* in Arabic, and refers to a fragrant, prized tree sap harvested from the bark of trees belonging to the genus *Styrax*.[18] Its smell is similar

18. "Lobana," Wisdom Library, last updated November 23, 2022, https://www.wisdomlib.org/definition/lobana.

to frankincense, and its smoke is believed to chase out even the harshest negative energy and malevolent spirits. Loban is a massively powerful cleanser that should be kept in any magickal practitioner's toolbox, especially for those who frequently work with the spirit realm.

In a sand-filled dish or bowl, light an incense charcoal outdoors. Once it becomes a glowing ember, place some loban resin on top and be prepared for a massive blast of cleansing smoke.

Walk through the area or areas you wish to cleanse, thoroughly getting the smoke in every cupboard, corner, and crevice. As you do so, loudly repeat the Greek phrase *Apo pantos kakodaimonis!*—"Away, every evil spirit!"

As you go about this process, or after you've wafted the smoke everywhere it's needed, consider ringing a bell or using a drum or shaker. Sound mixes up energy; the louder the better. Finish with a resounding, "Cleansed, cleared, and fortified!"

Repeat this working as necessary and integrate it with additional spells or rituals that specifically target your personal situation concerning unwelcome spirits and unwanted vibrations. Be sure to open any doors or windows so the energy can be chased *out*!

Extracting Energetic Leeches

It's very much possible to unintentionally pick up parasitic energies or entities in our daily lives. These can be anything from vampiric spirits to invisible creatures wandering on the astral plane looking to feed. Personally, I've inadvertently attracted these after going to certain bars or clubs, sketchy areas of unfamiliar cities, the homes of those suffering addiction (including hoarding), and locations densely haunted by hungry spirits. Astral leeches also try to attach from a person to another person, especially if they are experiencing a bad trip, a disassociating high, or a drunk episode. These leeches can also become attached when people interact with others in a distraught state and even during counseling, magickal, or therapeutic sessions if the provider is not properly protected.

Energetic leeches and parasites normally go under the conscious radar, but many people who are energetically sensitive or psychic can pick up on these attachments. Try this if you think one is trying to feed on your life force.

To halt external parasitic energy before it gets to feed, thereby depleting or disorienting your energy, cast it off by shouting at it. Demand that it detach from your energy, forcefully commanding that it's *not* allowed to feed. Scream and yell if you must. Be strong and send it away in your own powerful words. As you do so, burn eucalyptus or wear it as an essential oil. Continue this for one week to ensure the parasite doesn't reattach. You may also choose to burn camphor in addition to or in place of eucalyptus, as both camphor resin and eucalyptus leaves are mentholated, which is where the potency lies.

If your leech is particularly strong, burn and sprinkle asafoetida powder. Also called *hing* in Indian cooking (it tastes amazing in a dish), asafoetida is a gum resin extracted from a plant related to the carrot family. Its potent, onion-like spell earned it the name "devil's dung," which is also a reference to its ability to chase out infernal, chthonic, and vampiric spiritual energy.

Releasing Energetic Interference (Guest Spell)

The following spell is written by my dear and multitalented friend Lisa Allen M. H. (Calantirniel), who I originally met during my days as a college radio and club DJ. She is a master herbalist, astrology expert, and dowser who specializes in clairchronance (clear timing). She is also a cofounder of The Way of Arda's Lore, a unique spiritual path centered on the mystical storytelling of J. R. R. Tolkien. Find her links at www .LinkTr.ee/TimingMagic.

This spell helps dissolve and remove misaligned, discordant energies whether from random or targeted entity attachments, parasitic cords and hooks from others (most of which aren't consciously placed), or unresolved trauma imprints. It also assists with curse removal and dissolving various types of programs from sources such as Otherworldly influence, undoing religious and societal collective programming, rewriting past life stories, and even resolving patterns from living family and ancestors. In the case of the latter, these imprints may have been designed for survival but are now outdated and inappropriate, even harmful. All of these anomalies can limit our potential for happiness and growth.

While this spell is very powerful, it is designed to allow gentleness in your release, so you don't go into what I call an after-spell crisis. See Raven's Shadow Reflection about paradox on page 82 for more information about this phenomenon.

Note that this spell is not designed to solve all of life's challenges, nor will it necessarily erase all energetic interference instantaneously. This working is most beneficial alongside shadow work you're already enacting and serves to keep your energy on its highest trajectory.

This working involves using an energetically cleared and charged pendulum or other freely swinging device to read energy movement. No psychic talent or experience with pendulum dowsing is necessary.

If you don't have access to a pendulum, you can use a necklace or even a brass key tied to a substantial length of cotton string, as long as it is weighted enough and can easily swing in all directions. Whatever you choose, let your intuition guide you, experiment with what works, and ensure that it feels good in your dominant hand.

The pendulum is an excellent tool for tapping into the energy field of All That Is, also called Source energy. Your body naturally does this already and knows the truth of all things at a subtle yet deep level. We've been taught to ignore this sense, which puts our shadow in charge. With deconditioning, practice, and trust, the pendulum allows you to naturally reconnect with this field of truth and accurately interpret its energy.

The deconditioning process is not just knowing how to connect to this field for answers, but also learning how to healthfully process emotions. When we get out of our own way, as the saying goes, it allows for accurate answers to come into light by way of the pendulum's swing. Over time, divinatory acts including pendulum dowsing actually open the practitioner to objective truth rather than being influenced by subjectivity, expectation, and earthly longing. It's best to realize that being aligned with absolute truth is infinitely more desirable than any specific desired result, because working from false information or hope doesn't help anyone, especially oneself.

This pendulum spell is also called a pendulum command, affirmation, or decree. For extra potency, write out both of the following declarations by hand and burn the papers upon completion.

Holding your pendulum or makeshift pendulum, ask it to swing in a widdershins (counterclockwise) manner to assist with your releasing. Once it's strongly spinning, take a deep breath and boldly state the following agreement between you and the Powers That Be:

I, [your name], hereby ground, trust,
and therefore allow myself to open fully to receive the deepest love
and highest vibrations of Source Energy and my guides
as I call in the perfect protection for this work.

As this pendulum spins counterclockwise,
I easily and effortlessly notice, release, and dissolve all misaligned,
discordant energies, collective or personal, cloaked or not,
from all levels, timelines, lifetimes, and genetic coding.

I easily and effortlessly cut away, remove and dissolve all
harmful cords of attachment, curses, negative programming,
false narratives, outdated contracts, soul pieces not belonging to me,
and all interference and anomalies that have no place
in my highest vibrational state, including but not limited to
[state challenges you wish to overcome].

I easily forgive myself and others, as love solves all.

And so it is!

Allow the pendulum to show it is done by asking it to swing forward and backward instead of in a circular manner. Allow as much time is needed, and let yourself process any feelings, emotions, or sensations that arise. When the pendulum responds in this fashion, ask it to now swing in a deosil (clockwise) manner, in order to invite new frequencies. Declare the following:

As this pendulum spins clockwise, I hereby enhance my grounding and protection, while I receive and integrate the absolute height of positive energies wherein I can easily yet effectively navigate my life.

These frequencies energize and balance my chakras, correct auric tears, close improper portals, dissolve prior access points, and effortlessly integrate any soul pieces that are ready to return.

These highest vibrational energies from Source may install light codes that bring about vitality, health, happiness, love, abundance, prosperity, wealth, and [*state any additional qualities*].

Protect this work and shield me from any attempts by lower energies to perpetuate old stories, as I return to my earthly life with ease and flow.

My challenges are hereby entirely handled by the Universe, and outdated energies are now transmuted. I am hereby gently and gracefully transformed—*now*! And so it is!

Once again, ask and allow the pendulum to show it is done by swinging forward and backward. Thank Source, your guides, guardians, and Otherworld helpers. Repeat this working as often as you feel the need!

Appeasing Mischievous Faeries

There are innumerable views and perspectives about the faery realm, spanning virtually all cultures in human history. Cross-cultural similarities are aplenty when studying descriptions and documentations of the fae. Benevolent winged sprites are only one among countless faery beings, and many are believed to be mischievous and/or malevolent.

Whether shiny things keep going missing or you believe you're being personally toyed with by local fae, try this two-part working.

First, gather offerings. If you have an idea of the type of fae from whom you need protection, consider what they would most enjoy. Standard offerings include honey, cream, flowers, bells, mirrors, and shiny metallic objects. Take your offering plate to where you've felt their presence the strongest and speak to them directly:

Faeries here, faeries there,
I bring these gifts, I do declare!
From evening shade to morning's dew,
Enjoy these offerings, they're all for you!
I ask that you now leave me be.
Please go frolic and be free!

For an added boost of protection, you can utilize the classical alchemical symbol for the metal iron, shown on the previous page. This can be drawn on a protection charm, house ward, or even on your body. Because iron as a material has long been known to repel harmful energies and malicious fae, it's only appropriate to incorporate its symbol.

Naturally, you can guard yourself by creating a charm of any type that includes the actual metal iron in some fashion. If possible, incorporate rowan berries, bark, or leaves—this tree is also called mountain ash or witch wood and is believed to allow benevolent faeries to pass while guarding against darker varieties.

Archangelic Rebalancing

If shadows have been too heavy to work with lately and you've been feeling unusually off-kilter, try tapping into the angelic realm. Modern love-and-light interpretations aside, angels—particularly archangels—are profoundly powerful allies that anyone of any background can safely work with.

If you're familiar with the Lesser Banishing Ritual of the Pentagram (LBRP), as popularized by the Golden Dawn, it will do the trick and is highly advised during times of need. For those unfamiliar, or who are looking for a quick realignment, give this a try. The words intoned are taken from the LBRP.[19]

If possible, burn pure frankincense resin *or* loban (benzoin), which are used for calling the angelic realm and keeping their influence nearby. Utilize the stone angelite in some manner, or wear hematite if you've been particularly ungrounded as of late.

After meditating for a few minutes, stand up and face the east. When intoning the opening and closing "IAO," a Jewish name of God/Spirit, place your hands in the *anjali mudra* (prayer position). While intoning the names of the archangels, simply have open arms.

Intone each name loudly and boldly:

IAO (eee-ahhh-ohhh)!
Before me, Raphael (Rahhh-fayyy-elll)
Behind me, Gabriel (Gahhhb-rayyy-elll)
To my right hand, Michael (Mihhh-kaiii-elll)
To my left hand, Auriel (Ohhh-reee-elll)
Hail and welcome, mighty archangels!
Please guard and protect me now and ever onward!
IAO (eee-ahhh-ohhh)!

Shadow & Your Spirit Team (Guest Spell)

The following spell is written by my special friend Wythe Sherwood. He and I met at Denver's Pagan Pride festival, where I was signing books, reading tarot, and performing a puja to Lord Ganesha. Wythe later

19. Kraig, *Modern Magick*, 50.

accompanied me on part of the next book tour and has been influential in my life in regard to healing internalized shame, living more healthfully, and more accurately perceiving life's experiences.

Some amount of discomfort is guaranteed in shadow work. The only greater discomfort comes from *not* doing the work! The inner shadow is often a filter, a choke point, an energetically limiting factor. The shadow is the threshold over which we attempt to quarantine thoughts, feelings, and truths that feel too shamefully dark or terrifyingly luminous to deal with consciously. If unacknowledged, the shadow becomes an artificial holding tank, a short-sighted, self-sabotaging, unsustainable divorce from the rhythms, cycles, and processes that constantly move through us. We are the architects of our own shadows; we are its making and unmaking.

For many people, the internal shadow contains a strong element of shame and/or fear; these emotions inhibit relationships and influence isolation. Internalized shame, as well as the fear of what others think, serve to isolate oneself from necessary, nourishing connections. Connection is medicine for isolation, and community is medicine for shame.

Being held in community can be awkward. It requires being open, seen, known, and vulnerable. Connection and community are not exclusively physical, and this ritual is meant to assist a practitioner in their shadow work by forging a bond with their personal nonphysical team.

You are an ecosystem within ecosystems and are thus never alone in shadow work. Your deepest and highest self is rooting for you to be the most you that you can be. You have healed, radiant ancestors who have worked on themselves and your lineage. They want you to succeed. You have more spirit guides than you possibly know, and they all delight in your wellbeing.

This ritual was inspired by my studies in Anderson Feri, the Unnamed Path, and ADF-style Druidry. Feel free to adapt it in ways that make sense to you. The goal is to recognize the broad categories of beings you are *already* in relationship with and to encourage even deeper communion. If you have specific named ancestors, spirit guides, deities, or land spirits you'd like to call in specifically, great. If not, working with them in a general sense is still powerful and has the potential to reveal connections previously unknown.

Set your ritual space. In your preferred method, cleanse, ground, center, and acknowledge the sacredness of the time and space you are in. You may wish to burn frankincense and light a candle whose color represents the unseen world to you.

Make offerings within your means, in terms of time and resources. Be reasonable, flexible, and creative. Let your intuition guide you; if you're not sure, just pick something. This is about relationship building, and that's an ongoing conversation.

Common kinds of offerings are food and beverages, tobacco, representations of the natural season, spontaneous or pre-created songs or poems, dancing or moving in ways that feel inspired, and elemental representations such as candles, incense, water, and crystals. You don't necessarily have to purchase anything to make an offering. Know that your focused time and attention and even your very breath can themselves be spiritual offerings.

Check in with divination to see if offerings have been accepted. Use your preferred system to give a yes, no, or maybe. I tend to check in collectively, but if you want to check specifically for the land, ancestors, and guides, go for it. If you get a no, switch up what you're offering and try two more times. Three consecutive no responses means to try again later. Sometimes my spirits want more of something, sometimes less. Sometimes they want my full attention and not a physical object.

Now commune with your team. Leave space for activities that are expressive and receptive. Try different things. Meditate silently. Go for a walk with open eyes, ears, and heart to receive messages. Perform divination. Talk or write to them. Share your heart. What are your fears? What are your joys? What do they need to know about you and your ongoing shadow work? Take your time in fully opening to the powers at hand.

Knowing that these relationships exist outside of this ritual and that this communication will continue, thank everyone who showed up and make sure to pay attention to where you notice their presence as you go about your daily life.

Again, by your preferred method, draw the ritual to a close.

Dispose of offerings in ways that feel appropriate in terms of time and manner. Journal the experience as you wish, and repeat as you feel called. Go forth in the knowledge that you are supported and have inbuilt, birthright access to an ecosystem of spirits that are on your side in shadow work and beyond, even if it's not always immediately comfortable!

Honoring Your Invisible Comrades

We all have spiritual comrades, even those of us who are unaware of or disbelieve in them due to lack of experience. Everyone has one or more spirit guides, and the form they take is different for everyone. Many spiritual practitioners believe that we all have one or more spirit animals as well, some cultures believing that we have one long-term spirit animal guide (as an Oversoul of the greater species), and others that come into our lives physically and/or invisibly for a relevant length of time.

No one's invisible community is exactly the same. Deities, ancestor spirits, and the dearly departed may also walk with us throughout our lives or for a period of time. We also carry an imprint of gods, goddesses, and deities with whom we work or pray to.

When you feel the call and ideally on a significant day like a sabbat, new or full moon, or even during an eclipse, or your birthday, map out ways you can honor your comrades.

Make a list of any length while meditating by candlelight. Write down the names of any deities whose image you have on your altar, throughout the home, or hanging on your wall. Make note of any departed friends, relatives, or pets whose photos (or fur or collars) you have, and who might still be walking with you in life from time to time. Take note of any spirit, ancestor, or entity you actively work with or who is likely to be present in your energetic sphere. If you know the names of your spirit guides or the species of spirit animal(s) that walk with you, write those down or simply write "spirit guides and animal guides."

Here's the most important part: You are *not* asking anything in return while honoring them in this working. Gratitude is a profoundly transformative frequency, and it is one that naturally and acutely aligns your deepest self with these sacred comrades.

Choose an appropriate offering for each. This could be anything from an apple to a cigar, from rosewater to a candle, from a scroll of poetry to the gift of music. Take time to think about what sort of gift each guide, spirit, entity, deity, angel, or ancestor (or groupings thereof) would most appreciate. If it is heartfelt and is appropriate to their culture and individual personalities, you're on the right track. Have fun deciding what you can offer everyone; there are few greater joys in life than the fun of gifting.

When you're ready, approach each individual force with utmost gratitude and reverence. Make your offerings slowly and decidedly, communicating to each as you would a beloved friend. Don't rush the process and don't ask for anything. Tell them the reasons why you are grateful for having them in your life. If you work with deities from various cultures, be sure to extend gratitude for the fact that they can comfortably share space alongside your other spiritual comrades from different backgrounds.

Once completed, declare the following to honor everyone in unison:

Beloved comrades on the inner planes!
I honor you all with deepest reverence and respect.
Thank you for guiding my life, my soul, and my journey.
As I walk this path, I am safe with you by my side.
Thank you for accepting these offerings from my heart.
My dear and sacred comrades, I am honored to honor you.

CHAPTER 11

Sleep & Subtle Realms

As the title suggests, this chapter of the book delves into realms of sleep, dreaming, and the astral plane. Beginning with a curse removal that uses astral projection, we then gently enter the realm of slumber.

Because we're working with energies of shadow, which itself encompasses the unseen planes, it's only appropriate to look at nightmares and how we can guard ourselves from these dreamy disturbances. Every level of our health is impacted by the quality and quantity of rest we're able to offer our bodies and brains.

The process of dreaming is highly symbolic, linking directly with our personal, internal shadow. After all, Carl Jung was renowned for his incredibly deep and influential work into both dreaming and the shadow self (see page 2).

This chapter closes with an entry about entheogenic ceremonies. While hallucinogenic and psychoactive substances are not everyone's cup of tea, readers who are curious to learn more can benefit from the information provided. Like all shadow work, the altering of consciousness—which includes meditation, dreaming, and astral travel—should not be approached with frivolity, but rather with utmost awareness.

Astral Projection Curse Removal

Unrecognized by modern science (for now), the astral plane is believed, in metaphysics, to be a world parallel to this one. It is said to house a direct imprint of the waking plane's energetic imprints, furniture and all, alongside a variety of beings and entities affixed to that plane—and those who journey between worlds.

The astral plane or astral world can be accessed through astral projection: an intentional separation of the consciousness from the physical body. Those skilled in this art report animals responding to one's nonphysical presence, an awareness of the surrounding environment, and a connection with disembodied entities.

The astral plane is believed to be a lower energetic plane, often an energetic imprint of the physical plane, rather than a plane of higher frequency. For this reason, energetic imprints such as curses or hexes, intentional or unintentional, tend to "settle" on the astral plane, from where these energies affect a person's wellness.

If you have been cursed or believe yourself to have been, begin by making an astral tea to combat this affliction, even if you don't know the source or why such energy has accumulated. Combine any amount of blue lotus, jasmine, mugwort, damiana, and skullcap; steep it until drinkable. After consuming, lay down to breathe slowly and deeply.

Sense the tea in your tummy, the herbal infusion awakening and charging your physical and nonphysical bodies. With your hands, work this energy in a spiral so that it encompasses your entire frame. Deep breaths continuing, allow your consciousness to hover slightly above your body. You may begin to perceive the surrounding space. Maintain awareness of the physical body, looking for anything that seems "off."

If you perceive an energetic blockage between you and the outside world, mentally repeat the word "disappear" while visualizing the blockage spiraling in a widdershins (counterclockwise) fashion, fueled by the herbal magick pulsing through your body and astral self.

Cast this energy to Mother Earth for composting. Visualize your body continuing to be surrounded by the tea's energetic boost while you slowly return to your physical frame. Finalize by performing energetic cleansing in any manner you feel appropriate.

Neutralizing Astral Attacks

In addition to the previous working, if you feel astrally or psychically attacked, intentionally or unintentionally, perform a "null and void" spell to stop a hex in its tracks.

You don't deserve to be fucked with. This spell can be of assistance alongside protective measures explored in this book's fourth chapter.

Purchase blueberries and place them in a bowl on your altar. Additionally, purchase a low-dose cannabis edible (recommended dose: one milligram). Cannabis connects one to the astral plane, and the essence of blueberry is said to lift and remove any curses at hand. If marijuana is illegal in your area (if that makes a difference), or if you're aversely sensitive to the herb, substitute a *hemp* tincture, gummy, or flower to connect with CBD; this still contains trace amounts of THC and does not alter the mind.

Hands held above the berries and edible, visualize them glowing in deep blue and violet colors while repeating these words for as long as you see fit:

Fruit of life and holy cannabinoid,
Evils against me are null and void.

Eat the berries and cannabis (or CBD) while performing cleansing with sacred smoke—ideally sage, frankincense, or dragon's blood—followed by a shower or bath. Repeat the verbal spell in your mind for as long as you wish, and consider writing the spoken words on a piece of paper you can burn after you feel the negativity has lifted.

To further mix up the energy and claim your own, move your body. Dance to music you enjoy, ideally something nonvocal and newly discovered!

Astral Travel Ointment

In addition to the ritual of jumping around crops atop broomsticks and pitchforks to help them grow, Celtic folk magick recognizes ye olde Witches' Flying Ointment. I examine and explore this thoroughly in my book *A Witch's Shadow Magick Compendium*.

Modern Witches and magickal practitioners don't need hallucinogenic or potentially toxic ointments to achieve astral travel or bilocation. Whatever your reasons for this, an ointment such as this can assist.

In a base of jojoba, almond, or mineral oil, add any combination of the oils or essences of blue lotus, cannabis, wormwood, mugwort, marjoram, valerian root, asparagus root, huckleberry, ginkgo, and poplar (namely the buds, called balm of Gilead). To your mixture, add a small stone of tiger's eye and/or jasper.

The carrier oil you choose should be used as a 10:1 ratio, meaning one drop of essential oil for every 10 drops of carrier oil. It's also good to note that oils tend to last the longest in dark or amber-colored glass jars.

Anoint this oil on your brow, heart, hands, and feet. After settling into your chosen method for inducing astral projection, sense the moon. Feel moonlight settling into every layer and level of your being. Allow this illumination to help your invisible body separate from the physical, still attached by an astral cord, and go about your business on the astral plane.

A Soporific Solid Sleep Pillow

Sleep and dreaming are, by their very nature, directly connected to the realm of shadow. Like the sun descends and the moon wanes, our bodies, minds, and spirits must rejuvenate with good, solid, restful sleep.

Insomnia cannot be solved in these pages, and my highest recommendation is to seek out herbal or medical treatment if this is your affliction. If your sleep has been unrestful lately in any manner, make a soporific pillow. This pillow can be a small sachet to keep beneath your regular pillow or can be something larger that you snuggle each night. Alternatively, keep this pillow or sachet tucked underneath your mattress.

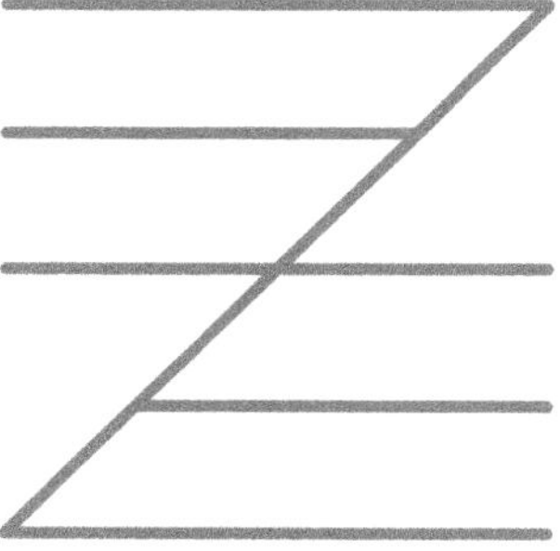

Determine the way in which you'll craft your pillow or sachet. You may instead or additionally wish to craft a meditation cushion, depending on your intention. The best herbs to incorporate in either or both of these cases are lavender, poppy seeds, kratom, frankincense, peppermint, and hops for sleepy vibes and protection in the dreamworld. For additional ingredient ideas, check out this book's Correspondences under "Dream Vision & Protection."

Add a small moonstone to the mix. Incorporate graveyard dirt or grave dust for an extra sleepy boost (see page 176). You may also wish to incorporate a tablet of melatonin or tryptophan inside your pillow. Additionally, use ink or a permanent marker to draw sleepy symbols (such as the one on the previous page) all over the pillow alongside swirls and any symbols related to the unconscious.

At dusk, go outside and hold your pillow to the setting sun in the west. Enchant the bag by declaring nine times (nine being the number of the moon in esoteric Qabalah):

Setting sun and restful dusk,
Charge this bag with sandman's dust.
The unconscious I glimpse and visions I keep,
This pillow is enchanted for restful sleep.

Guarding Against Nightmares

Nightmares suck. They are disturbing and can stick with us for the majority of a day. The mind scares itself, bringing to light shadowed themes that beg to be recognized.

Before bed, drink a tea of vervain and mugwort, both of which guard against nightmares. The most powerful ingredients to additionally combine with this tea are the herbs thyme, mullein, anise, and purslane. (Do not drink mugwort, wormwood, or any member of the Asteraceae family if you are pregnant, have chronic GI issues, or are taking an anticoagulant. If there is any question about contraindications, consult an herbalist before consuming.)

The aforesaid herbs can be brewed into a tea, and can also be added to a sachet or pillow specifically for the purpose of guarding against nightmares. Additional herbs renowned for this purpose include hops, rue, hyacinth, and mullein. Also, a sprig of rosemary beneath the pillow is alleged to do the same. The ideal stones to include are topaz, chalcedony, and chrysolite. See this book's Correspondences for additional alignments under "Nightmares, to stop."

Also consider purchasing an authentic dream catcher from a crafter who is Native American; local Reservations and Etsy are both great sources for this. If purchased, you can "boost" the dream catcher by affixing feathers from any bird along with a snakeskin shed, a holey stone, a small abalone shell, and/or beads of genuine moonstone.

You may also wish to place a mirror underneath your bed, facing upward where your heart or head is positioned. Surround the mirror with salt for an added boost of dreamtime protection. Also, ensure no mirror directly faces your bed, as this can cause personal energy to accumulate with nowhere to disperse.

After drinking your tea and/or affixing your protective dream amulet, when you are settling into bed, softly chant the words, "safeguarded and protected" both as a whisper and in your mind as you drift into slumber.

Shaking a Bad Dream

Bad dreams—nightmares, for all intents and purposes—can stay with a person for a long time. When the subconscious mind is processing deep experiences and sensations, we can wake up overwhelmed with the nightmare's memory and a lasting psychological imprint. We need to ensure these impressions don't negatively influence our daily life. The brain interprets dreaming experiences as real, and we are lucky to have inbuilt amnesia after dreams—*and* after past lives.

The best remedy is grounding and centering: grounding into this reality here and now, and centering your thoughts into your body.

If you have a dream journal, write it down. If you don't have a dream journal, this is the perfect opportunity to create one.

After recording your upsetting dream, as soon as you can go outside of the house, touch the earth with your fingertips. Take deep breaths and come back to center. Cry if you need to, all tears becoming offerings to Mother Earth.

Stretch your left hand upward to invoke cosmic light while your right hand touches the safety of Earth. Visualize and feel the cosmic and earthbound energy entering you simultaneously. Breathe deeply and let this center your mind and spirit.

Follow up by brewing your morning cup of coffee, tea, or warm elixir. Hold your hands above the cup and visualize the shape of an eye atop the cup. If it's not too hot, use your pointer finger to draw this shape to help stimulate the *ajna* (brow) chakra.

If the dream you had was deeply disturbing, burn cedar or cypress, which are known to help calm the mind and purify mental impressions. Wear hematite bracelets or place a stone of hematite in each pocket to further ground and center throughout the day.

A Dream Vision Spell

It can be revelatory, if not overwhelming, to receive a message in the dreamworld. Not everything we perceive there is significant, as the unconscious is working out various stimuli in abstract form while the physical body rejuvenates and regenerates. Still, sometimes the messages are meaningful, and can inspire anything from personal change to creative pursuits.

Prophetic dreams are those that deliver that very thing: prophecy. These are more rare, as the ability to predict the future is notoriously vague for most people, but this spell may also influence these to occur.

To inspire the reception and recollection of messages in the dreamworld, the following actions are the most renowned for inducing this. I've gathered these methodologies from references encompassing various times and cultures, so do what you feel is best, and work with what you have available.

Inside a pouch or soft bag, place mugwort with a piece of moonstone and labradorite underneath your pillow or at the bedside. Another stone for helping receive dreamtime messages is garnet. The best herbs to incorporate are bay leaf, jasmine, and flaxseed. Comfrey and rosemary may be utilized to help consciously remember dreams. You may also choose to burn a mixture of copal, mugwort, and mastic in your bedroom, safely extinguishing the incense charcoal before slumber. A dream journal is highly suggested, within which you can write your dreams immediately upon waking; this allows you to examine and explore dreamtime imagery later in the day.

Drink a warm glass of unsweetened coconut milk or jasmine tea immediately before bed. After lying down, focus on the dreamy ingredients you've selected for your spellcraft. Envision your body's energy connecting with the herbal and mineral components, and then say the following simple phrase out loud nine times, before repeating it over and over in your mind as you drift off:

Dreamtime give me vision, memory, and precision.

Sending a Message by Dream (Guest Spell)

The following spell is written by Brett Hedgepath (Cory Valerian). He and I met when he visited my hometown of Missoula, Montana. I was jointly operating a Pagan temple at the time, and we quickly became lifelong friends. Brett is a Witch with a penchant for dream magick, and I'm pleased to include his fantastic offering here.

Occultists recognize the importance of dreams as something to be analyzed, remembered, and in which to participate. Dreams can pave the way to many forms of magick, including energy healing, spirit work, and divination. *Oneiromancy,* or dream interpretation, is possibly the oldest form of divination. Dreams take place in a seemingly externalized setting made to represent our current state of mind. Interpreting one's dreams is a great way to develop intuition. Dreams recharge the psychic centers and revitalize personal power.

The following Germanic-based spell is used to send a message to someone in a dream. Sometimes traditional methods of sending messages are unavailable or ineffective. The intended recipient may be somewhere unreachable by phone or mail. Maybe the message you want to send is very personal or too intimate to write out or say over the phone.

This spell is taken from my personal Book of Shadows. It was originally inspired by an entry in Judika Illes' brilliant *Encyclopedia of 5000 Spells*, and contains my own additions and modifications.[20] I have successfully used it to convey to a friend how much I missed them after having moved back to my hometown. I didn't know how to get in contact with them, but soon after working the spell, we were able to make contact. They were drawn to seek out my

20. Judika Iles, *The Element Encyclopedia of 5000 Spells: The Ultimate Reference Book for the Magical Arts* (HarperElement, 2004), 354.

email address after having a dream about me; one that I projected to them.

Determine the exact message that needs to be sent by way of dream. On the night of a new moon, place a clear quartz crystal and a naturally-made hagstone (holey stone) in a glass of spring water or well water. Leave this outside overnight. At the start of the waxing moon, put fresh sheets on your bed and sprinkle a little of the water on your bed each night while focusing on the message you wish to send.

As you sprinkle the water, walk deosil (clockwise) around your bed while speaking the following chant in German. This translates to "This dream is for you, to receive my message. And so it shall be:"

Dieser Traum ist für Dich,
um meine Nachricht zu erhalten.
Und so soll es sein.

At the first quarter half-moon, place herbs for dreaming in a cheesecloth sachet. This can include any combination of poppyseed, yarrow, dittany of Crete, thyme, mugwort, vervain, and aloeswood (also called agar or oudh). Hold the bag in your left hand, concentrating on the person to whom you're sending the dream. Place this sachet inside your pillowcase. Each night until the full moon, visualize the dream as you fall asleep.

When the lunar cycle is complete, change the sheets again to end the "transmission" of the dream message and to signal to your higher self that the spell is complete.

Preparing for an Entheogenic Ceremony

Entheogens are psychoactive, hallucinatory, or psychedelic substances or compounds ingested to create vision, insight, expanded awareness, and healing on emotional and spiritual levels. The ceremonial usage of such medicines is entirely different from recreational drug use.

Entheogens have been used ceremonially since the dawn of humankind, with each substance having a distinct personality and bringing a unique experience to the individual. Each medicine comes to the experiencer with messages and guidance about what a person needs.

Examples of entheogens include psilocybin (magick mushrooms), peyote, ayahuasca, San Pedro cactus, iboga, and even cannabis (marijuana) when used in ceremony. Some healers also work with chemical teachers like MDMA (ecstasy), DMT, LSD, and ketamine.

One should approach an entheogenic experience with serious and mature awareness, and follow the invitation *from* the psychoactive medicine to sit with it when (and if) the calling and synchronicity occur. This is a deeply personal psychospiritual decision; not something to engage in for the sake of getting high or satisfying the ego. One should thoroughly prepare and reflect before undertaking an entheogenic ritual.

The set and setting of the experience, as well as the plan for its duration, should be explicitly determined and agreed upon in advance. It's best to undertake these potentially intense journeys with an experienced guide. Professional guides are trained and certified in facilitating entheogenic medicine. Guided ceremonies are deeply valuable, but certainly are not a requirement for sitting with any given medicine. In short, keep safe company with whom you can journey in perfect love and perfect trust.

One's local laws should be taken into consideration, and utmost caution should precede an entheogenic trip. A health screening is advised, and one should know of any and all potential contraindications (adverse reactions) before ingesting a psychoactive substance. Safety is a priority on every level!

If applicable for your setting, a notebook and pen are suggested, as are artistic books, creative supplies, and an array of items that are spiritually sentimental to you personally. Each situation will be different, so be sure to prioritize your comfort. A warm blanket and water are also recommended! If at any time you feel discomfort, remember the phrases "what we resist persists" and "the only way out is through."

To quote my dear and longtime friend Susan Morse (www.rootgirlsound.com), who is an experienced sound healer and entheogenic facilitator,

"When we are called to sit with entheogenic medicine, as soon as we decide to heed that call, we open a portal for plant spirit to reach out with messages. With that in mind, we should pay attention to our dreams both leading up to and following our journey. Take time to set an intention and prepare for the journey with respect and an open heart. We should also honor our bodies in the weeks leading up to our journey by eating clean foods, drinking water and herbal teas, and abstaining from alcohol, caffeine, sugar, animal proteins, and other products as instructed. Many facilitators will encourage you to try a *dieta*, which is a practice in getting to know an herb, like rose or basil, and inviting it to come to know you, as you prepare for this potentially life-changing entheogenic experience."[21]

21. Susan Morse, personal interview, March 2025.

If you have, for your own personal reasons, arranged an entheogenic experience with a wholly trustworthy person or persons, and if it's permitted with the medicine, brew a cup of holy basil tea, set a clear intention, speak to the infusion, and drink the tea before ingesting the entheogenic medicine as described below. This tea is relaxing but not psychoactive. Also called *tulsi* in India, holy basil is a prized and respected plant, and is known to instill courage before an initiation. Entheogenic journeys are quite often initiatory experiences, especially in ceremonial settings.

Note that if you are undertaking this experience with a trained facilitator, many discourage anything but fresh water in the fast leading up to the ceremony, and as part of their prescribed *dieta*. If this is the case for you, choose to sit with tulsi on the days leading up to the ceremony, but abstaining on the day itself. (I suggest the gorgeous tea Tulsi Sweet Rose by Organic India.)

Cup your hands over the tea and, before drinking, speak the following words to the infusion:

Herbal ally, sacred medicine, holy basil,
Please guard my visionary experience.
As I journey to unseen worlds of mind and spirit,
May I be filled with bravery and safety.

CHAPTER 12

Death & the Afterlife

This twelfth and final chapter takes a look at shadow as expressed by death energy, with the opening spell exploring the mystical and emotional desire to leave one's body before its time. To most successfully work with death energy, we must first bring to light our own personal perspectives of and relations with death, dying, and the afterlife.

Some shadow workers are highly sensitive to the realm of the dead and can make excellent psychic mediums if the ability is controlled. Other practitioners are more empathic or traditionally psychic, while others have great acuity with arts of physical healing. Whatever one's inborn skills and spiritual callings, we all have some amount of access to the afterworld because those very planes are connected to life itself.

We all have ancestors, whether those recently deceased or those whose footprints remain in the sands of time. A number of spells and rituals offered here suggest methods of honoring and working with our ancestors and those who have gone before us.

Themes of working with ghosts, hauntings, and even past lives wrap up this book's final chapter. Its conclusion is a funerary rite for laying one's own past to rest.

Just as the sun is reborn daily and the moon reborn monthly, and just as tree leaves fall and become fertilizer for a subsequent cycle of growth, it would be foolish to think that consciousness itself is an exception to nature's cyclical reality. Working with death energy can help us become more gentle, more reverent, and grateful to be alive.

Easing Spiritual Homesickness

As we've explored, many people drawn to shadow work are prone to depression. Sometimes this manifests in thoughts of spiritual homesickness; a longing to leave the body and return to Source. These thoughts are normally fleeting, and it's not uncommon for mystical people to feel a sense of spiritual disconnection at times. We are but fractal fractures of infinite spirit temporarily embodying beautiful and often complicated physical frames; the ego and mind included.

If these thoughts are weighing heavily on your mind and affecting your quality of life, especially if they're accompanied by suicidal ideation or dangerous escapist tendencies, please seek immediate medical assistance. We don't deserve to experience hopelessness, and there are a tremendous amount of resources available, many free of charge, from psychologists to therapists to counselors to life coaches, and so much more. Keep a list of your local crisis phone numbers and text lines should you or someone you know need immediate support. We must be our own advocates because we're here for a reason and life is already short as is. Fight for your happiness! This spell can help alongside other methods of working with the longing to return home.

Facing your altar in darkness, light a green candle. Place the Wheel of Fortune card from your favorite tarot deck on the center of your altar; if you have multiple decks, take that same card from four decks, as four is the number of Jupiter (the card's planetary ruler).

Place a dead and dried sand dollar (a type of sea urchin) between the candle and card(s). If you have a carnelian, place this on your altar or wear it as a charm, as it is known to dispel depression and increase confidence.

Prepare a tool and method for smashing open the sand dollar. When this happens, approximately five "doves" will be released that are part of the creature's skeletal remains. These dovelike figures have come to represent freedom, peace, and spiritual assurance.

Get comfortable and look at the Wheel of Fortune card or cards illuminated by candlelight. Hold the dried sand dollar at your heart. Study the card's details in depth, as you realize that it's telling you to hold on; life isn't always a pleasant experience, but you will be lifted back up. With four deep inhalations, absorb the essence of the sand dollar and Wheel of Fortune card, feeling their properties of uplifting reassurance.

Before smashing open the sand dollar, hold it to the card(s) and candle, declaring:

Light of life, my mind has been dim.
I long for Oneness but know I must be here now.
Tarot. Rota. Wheel of Life. Lift me up!
Evolution! Growth and regeneration, I am yours!

Keep me safe in this body and mind.
Ease this longing, quiet these thoughts.
By the breaking of this shell, may I be at peace in my own!
Please bless my long life with health and with strength.
For someday I shall return to your arms in bliss.

Kiss the sand dollar and then carefully smash it open. Marvel at its perfectly-formed contents. Keep the doves on your altar or use them in charms, artwork, or in any manner you're guided to honor their inspiring magick, and keep your head up as you more confidently engage with whatever life has to offer! It's a blessing to be here now.

Dedicating an Ancestral Altar

Shadow practitioners are naturally attuned to energies of the Otherworld, including the realm of spirit guides, ancestors, and the beloved dead. It's only appropriate that we honor those who have gone before us, particularly if their teachings and influence strongly resonate with us.

We can honor those who preceded us by creating and dedicating a shrine specifically for the ancestors. The focus the shrine is entirely up to each practitioner. Some ancestral shrines venerate people and pets we personally knew. Others honor ancestors of the land one resides on, or ancestors of their personal lineage. Still other shrines honor one's departed guru or gurus, holy people, and ascended masters. An ancestral shrine can focus on any or all of these individuals.

Make room for an ancestral shrine or select a designated spot on a greater altar. Decide what the focus of your shrine will be. Is it to honor one specific soul or a number of souls? Ancestors you knew personally or those you never had the pleasure of meeting in person? Meditate and see what resonates with your heart. Then get images of each individual or something that represents them.

Next, gather a new, long-lasting candle intended specifically for the shrine. Make sure it's one you can ignite and extinguish regularly. If appropriate to your style of altar, incorporate objects that belonged to them in life. Add their favorite foods and drinks, not forgetting to rotate them regularly—don't let offerings become moldy!

Once you've added everything you can think of to honor the individual or individuals, conclude by adding a living plant. This can be any plant of your choosing, and should be consistently maintained. The inclusion and offering of something living is a profound offering to those whose spirits have departed their earthly vessels.

On a dark moon or a significant evening of your choosing, light the dedicated candle and slow your breath. Touch the living plant with your right hand and then your heart. Focus on each soul represented on the altar. When ready, communicate with each of them directly, stating the purpose for your shrine. If you wish, dedicate the shrine as a whole to archangel Azrael, to a deity of death and rebirth, or to familiar spirits of choice.

Ideally, choose one day of the week or month to spend time with your ancestral altar. If choosing a specific day of the week, Saturday is recommended due to its rulership of Saturn. If you choose one time each month, the dark or new moon is naturally best.

Don't overthink your ability to commune with the beloved dead; just assure that everything you do comes from the heart and may very well be clearly heard and received. Upkeep the altar regularly and with reverence. Keep in mind that we, too, will become ancestors one day. At some point, it will be our own photo on a shrine!

Preparing to Work with the Dead

There are many reasons for a person to work with those who have gone before us, including simply honoring and speaking to those we love who have crossed over. Any serious practitioner who works with death energy does so with deepest reverence and humility. We don't command or attempt to control spirits unless there's a potentially dangerous haunting situation. When communing with the departed or dealing with death energy in general, the wise practitioner approaches from a place of respect.

At this point in time, *necromancy* is a term that goes beyond "divination by means of communicating with the dead."[22] A great many practitioner of necromantic arts use the term to refer to any method of working with spirits on the other side, including mediumship. For our purposes, I'll shy away from the term and simply mention working with the dead.

For a deeper dive into death magick, please check out Christian Day's *The Witches' Book of the Dead* and Tomás Prower's *Morbid Magic: Death Spirituality & Culture From Around the World* (see bibliography).

Additionally, please look at the correspondences under the "Spirit Work" category in order to determine if you'd like to integrate any of those associated plants, gemstones, and other items into this working or others similar.

To prepare yourself to communicate with the dearly departed however you see fit and whatever method is most comfortable, you can cleanse and align your body and mind with some magick in advance.

Prepare the space by burning a combination of copal and myrrh. Slow down your actions and intentionally slow your breath.

---

22. Greer, *Encyclopedia of the Occult*, 324.

Move and breathe in this way to connect your energy with the Otherworld, where time moves differently and energies are subtle.

Strip nude (skyclad) and hug your body. Give thanks to your body as the unique vessel in which your soul rests at this time. Slowly enter the shower and, before turning on the water, pour at least one cup of pomegranate juice all over your body after taking a sip.

As the juice drips from head to toe, state this or something similar:

Purified by the blood of my ancestors,
I approach the Great Beyond protected and aware.

After solemnly showering off, approach the space in which you'll be working with death energy. Wear a black or white robe or cloak if possible, and be sure to incorporate an amethyst in your workings with death energy. Stay safe, work within your comfort zone, and get some good solid sleep afterward!

A Cemetery Crossroads Releasing

Crossroads and cemeteries are both liminal spaces; thresholds between one place and another. A crossed road inside a cemetery or graveyard is especially liminal, allowing us to stand on the precipice of this world and the next.

This spell honors the dead while also assisting the caster in laying certain things to rest.

Cut a sheet of parchment paper into four rectangles. Write the names or symbols of the four terrestrial elements on the paper, that is, one on each page: earth, air, fire, and water. Bring to mind a number of associations with each element that you'd like to release from your life. For example, you may wish to banish instability by way of earth, overthinking by way of air, impulsivity by way of fire, sadness by way of water, and so on. List as many challenging feelings as you'd like.

On a night then the moon is full, visit a cemetery crossroads. Privately offer an apple, a handful of any grain, and a shiny silver coin in the middle of the crossroads. Say a whispered prayer to the spirits of the departed.

Next, burn one piece of paper to each appropriate direction, starting in the west (water) and working widdershins (counter-clockwise) to the south (fire), the east (air), and finish with the north (earth).

Once again face west and declare in your own words that you've hereby laid to rest negative and unhelpful aspects of your life. Once again give thanks to any spirits that may be present as well as to your own spiritual guardians and higher self.

Take a deep, heartfelt bow to the west and walk away without looking back.

Processing Another's Death

Grief and mourning are not linear processes of healing that we experience to reach the end goal of acceptance. The grieving process looks different for everyone, and emotions are prone to fluctuate between all the stages or phases of grief for an unpredictable length of time. The sadness of loss doesn't always see closure, but somehow we learn to carry on.

The fact that we can experience immense pain at the loss of someone we love is an indication that we had the blessing, the pleasure, and the privilege of experiencing love with them in this lifetime. Those are the deepest moments of spiritual sharing. Loving bonds are not to be avoided because of the inevitable separation. Our bonds keep us mutually supported because we all need each other throughout the trying experience of life on this plane.

If your grief is strong and long-lasting, please consider seeing a grief counselor or a therapist experienced in helping clients process the sorrow of loss. We are all in it together, and we deserve to both offer and receive support during times of difficulty. Take care of yourself by opening up to support on any level.

When mourning the loss of a human or animal, whether or not you knew them personally (for example, the loss of a notable influential person), write a sincere letter to the spirit of the departed soul or souls. If possible, have their photograph or a representation of them nearby while you write your words. If choosing an incense, opt for myrrh and/or sandalwood.

Take this letter to the base of one of the trees or shrubs listed here. These are all spiritually associated with helping a person connect with the dearly departed in various cultures: acacia, alder, apple, cypress, elder, holly, myrtle, oak, pomegranate, poplar, weeping willow, and yew.

Underneath the tree, read your letter aloud, burn it, and make any offerings as you see fit. Allow emotions to flow while performing this, knowing that your message is heard and your own spirit is consoled by the tree's regenerative comfort.

Helping Spirits Cross Over

The Greek word *psychopomp* refers to those who conduct souls to the afterworld. These are certain deities, spirits, and even humans who have the skill of helping souls of the dead move on to their next evolution and/or assist the dying in preparing for death in order to assure as peaceful a transition as possible. Death doulas, hospice workers, morticians, and others who regularly work with death energy may also consider themselves psychopomps of sort.

Even if it's not your specialty or calling in life, everyone has the ability to help guide souls to the afterlife. This spell is designed to assist those who have *already* crossed over, including earthbound disincarnate spirits (ghosts) you did not know personally in life. Additionally, this is a *pleasant* working, not one to banish harmful entities.

Henbane is one of the most renowned herbs for working with the dead. Handle this plant carefully due to its toxicity, and substitute a different nightshade (from the Solanaceae family) if you're unable to acquire henbane specifically.

In a safe ritual space, call upon your spirit guides to ask for protection and insight. Surround yourself with henbane or wear a sachet containing the herb. Burn boneset, myrrh, and/or sandalwood, all of which are believed to help spirits move onward and away from limbo.

Bring to mind the spirit or spirits you're encouraging to cross over. Speak to them directly, and don't second-guess their ability to perceive you. Speak loudly and firmly, using their name or names. In your own words, tell them that they have died and are now on the other side.

During this process, your intuition and instincts will become heightened. Listen to your inner voice and determine which points you wish to reiterate multiple times. For example, you may be inclined to tell the spirit or spirits to "go to the light" or "find the light," or you may instinctively know to inform the spirit multiple times that they have died and need to move on. Call upon *their* guides and ancestors, asking that they assist them in moving on. Depending on your proximity in life to the departed, you may have personal messages that deserve to be reiterated. Know that you are heard.

Close the space as you wish and give thanks to those in attendance. Ring bells and chimes if you find it helpful—you may even wish to sing!

Repeat the working if necessary, and ensure that you remain spiritually safe after having merged your personal energy with that of the afterlife. See protection spells and rituals in this book as well as those in other spellbooks if needed. Stay safe and know that you performed good, necessary work. After all, if we were the ones stuck on the other side, a little support from the living would be greatly appreciated!

A Sachet Against Hauntings

Drawstring sachet bags and similar charms are used in magickal work across numerous cultures. The ingredients for this particular bag are all used for protection against unwanted energies and entities.

Sachets can be hung up in a particular location or can be carried on person in the case of a spirit or ghost trying to attach itself to you personally.

Place any combination of the following in your sachet before sealing it shut: salt, garlic powder, onion powder, camphor, asafoetida (hing), sulfur (brimstone), anvil dust (a byproduct of blacksmithing), and black tourmaline. Incorporate the metal iron in any form. See this book's correspondences for further ingredient ideas under the category "Spirits, to protect against."

For an added boost, burn the herb boneset and run the bag through its smoke. This smoke can also be wafted in haunted areas in need of cleansing. Envision the bag glowing with the brightest light you can muster. Present the sachet to all four directions, then above and below. Take time to visualize the sachet's deflective light growing so strong that it makes your hands tingle. Repeat this visualization as often as you see fit (ideally during full moons) and carry or place it anywhere you sense harmful forces at play. Integrate this spell with others or in a greater protective ritual if you see fit.

Glimpsing into Past Lives

Past lives are a fascinating topic. Just as we see nature regenerating seasonally, planets cycling around us, and our body's own rhythm of sleep and wakefulness, it only makes sense that consciousness also works in a cyclical pattern.

One of the primary concerns of past lives is the ego, perhaps most prominently explored in the Buddhist concept of *anatta* or *anatman* ("no self"), which begs the question to what extent we "are" the person (or animal) from our many past lives. Buddhist philosophy additionally explores the idea of *anicca* ("impermanence") and may be one of the best lenses under which to theorize about the intricacies of reincarnation.

Many readers of this book will have some awareness of their own past life experiences, or may have inclinations based on present-day preferences, curiosities, challenges, fears, talents, recurring life lessons, and other potential carryovers. The simple magickal act presented here may very well help one uncover deeper experiences and insights associated with the soul's cycle of rebirth.

On the night of a dark moon, situate yourself comfortably in darkness. Allow one candle to illuminate a mirror before you, placed in a position that allows you to sit comfortably with a pillow on your lap while gazing into your own eyes. Determine the best place for the candlelight and ensure that there is minimal illumination in your reflection.

Make use of any of the following herbs in any way you see fit, all of which are renowned for achieving past life regression: rosemary, bay leaves, honeysuckle, lilac, and juniper. You may also wish to include bloodstone, tiger's eye, or any type of fossil (including petrified wood and ammonite) for the same purpose. See "Past Life Regression" in this book's correspondences for further ideas and suggestions for substitutions.

Blur your eyes and slow your breathing. Gaze into your eyes in the mirror's reflection and don't forget to blink! As you do so, repeat in a whisper and in your mind:

Lifetimes I've experienced, appear to me now.

Clear your mind and allow visions to appear on top of the vision of your reflection. Allow emotions to come naturally, as they will also be providing a direct link to your spiritual past. You can ask any given vision of a lifetime to reveal itself to you in more detail.

You're most likely to receive meaningful past life visions relevant to your current incarnation. These will be heightened experiences in any given lifetime, such as marriages, labor, rituals, sexual experiences, dying, and even glimpsing former scenarios with individuals you know in this current lifetime. You may see yourself experiencing a variety of ages, sexes, cultures, and worldviews. If the insights get too intense or come too quickly, take a deep breath and move your body before diving back in.

Don't hesitate to close your eyes on occasion to check for any visions that way. Journal your experience afterward and eat something nourishing to help ground and center back into your present space-time.

A Funeral for the Past

Working with death energy is not restricted to working directly with spirits of the deceased, ancestral forces, or deities who oversee death and dying. We can also work with death energy and connect to our experiences of it within this lifetime.

Facing, accepting, and moving on from difficult experiences allow us to get a smile back on our face and to invoke a bit of hope when it's needed most. Laying the past to rest is actually a daily process; things rarely happen overnight. Each day gives us a renewed opportunity to align with higher callings, deeper self-awareness, and better life choices.

To assist the process of moving on from traumatic experiences and unhealthy recurring cycles, choose an evening of a full moon or waning moon to intently focus your energy. Procure a snakeskin shed or another creature's molt specifically for this spell.

In a comfortable, cleansed, sacred space, light a black candle and a natural incense of your choosing. Bring to mind the traumas, bad choices, and discomforts of the past. With every exhale, feel as if you're pushing those feelings into the shed until you can feel it fully engulfed with your intention.

When ready, hold the snakeskin before you and boldly declare the following:

Ashes to ashes, dust to dust,
To leave behind the past I must.

With hardship solved and lessons learned,
A bright future comes as this snakeskin is burned.

Carefully ignite and burn the snakeskin with the candle's flame. Place these ashes along with graveyard dirt (see page 176) and herbs of your choice in a tissue or a small, biodegradable makeshift cardboard coffin (don't use tape).

Dress yourself in black, ideally veiled, to oversee a silent funeral somewhere in nature. Try to go somewhere you aren't likely to remember, as you will not need to revisit. Once you're there, make a small hole in the earth, place the coffin inside, and cover it with soil. Say your final prayers and thank your guardian spirits. Leave an offering suitable for animals in the area as you also give thanks to the local spirits and your own spiritual guides.

Pay attention to the subsequent lunar cycle (dark to full) for an excellent opportunity to invoke energies of renewal, rebirth, and reassurance. Use this period of time to invite whatever is antithetical to what you laid to rest in the waning tide.

May each passing day present new opportunities for working with the shadow for the greater good.

Conclusion

Throughout the course of this book, you've been reminded of familiar concepts and have learned new pieces of wisdom that pertain to your life's experience. You've been given the opportunity to think about the force of shadow in numerous ways. Being linked to the unconscious, the liminal, and the invisible, shadow work and shadow magick help us become more self-aware and more spiritually complete.

I invite you to regularly refer to this book of spells, charms, and rituals, utilizing its concepts and practices as the needs arise. You might end up transferring some of the spells and correspondences to your personal magickal journal or Book of Shadows. You may end up using this book as a reference to assist others with their own shadow work. Perhaps you'll formally or informally educate others in some of these esoteric concepts throughout your own personal or professional life.

Although this book is unique in its approach to shadow, my process of creating the book as an author followed a similar pattern to books and decks I've co-created in the past. I didn't set out to make a spellbook with such a wide range of shadow-based techniques and procedures, but the information was, in part, transmitted to me for creative interpretation and presentation. As a result of (sometimes exhaustingly) surrendering to the Powers That Be, the book ended up taking a far more curious and expansive final form than originally envisioned—and I'm perfectly happy with that!

Being the reader, experiencer, and practitioner, I encourage your own reinterpretations of the material throughout. You may choose to interpret and customize a number of these workings based on your personal needs and by making use of your own moral compass—or should I say *mortal* compass?! You are the center of your world, and your own internal shadow work comes first and foremost. From the vantage point of honest inner-work, your magickal and ceremonial actions are sure to be more accurate, successful, and deeply felt.

Our actions sow karmic seeds and have an impact on the world at large, both visible and invisible, in ways both small and mighty. Your work in this world is of great importance, and it all begins with yourself. By sitting with and working with your own shadow, you can more acutely work with others, and harness an evolutionary echo of influence in this lifetime and beyond.

It's my hope that you will add to, expand, and fine-tune these workings for the benefit of yourself and the world around you. This book is designed to be a helper along the way, providing a curated selection of workings for your consideration. This series of spells and contemplations invite you to adjust, adapt, and adopt. It's what you do with the information that counts, and the true essence of magick is in the heart of the caster.

May you be empowered, safe, and wise throughout life's adventure. Be true to yourself and remember that love is the key to it all. I am glad you exist.

In shadow and light, namaste and blessed be,

Raven Digitalis
Samhain, 2025

Correspondences

The following is a reverse lookup for a variety of herbs, plants, trees, incenses, gemstones, minerals, animal parts, curios, and other components for purposes frequently utilized in shadow magick. A variety of material correspondences are listed together by metaphysical purpose and are not divided into subcategories.

These are some of the most potent or most renowned material correspondences for various magickal purposes relevant to shadow work, but is by no means an end-all-be-all. The spells in this book do not suggest using *all* of the following ingredients in each spell for any given purpose, so this reference may also be used for substitutions.

This list does not suggest specific ways in which to use any given ingredient, so, as always, exercise caution. Don't ingest anything you're not familiar with or that's not designed for consumption. Some things listed that are sometimes ceremonially consumed (psychoactive mushrooms, for example) don't necessarily need to be eaten for magickal purposes, but can instead be used and attuned externally, like added to a spell bag or incorporated in a piece of art.

Readers may wish to add to these lists based on one's own research and experience, and even consider copying select correspondences into a personal Book of Shadows or magickal journal.

Correspondences, Alignments & Substitutions

Addictions, to break

Amethyst
Catnip
Frankincense
Eucalyptus
Hyssop
High John the Conqueror
Ivy
Lavender
Lemongrass
Mullein
Nightshade
Pepper, black
Sage
Vinegar
Wormwood

Anger, to calm

Dandelion
Ice
Passionflower
Peridot
Quartz, rose
Wormwood

Anxiety, to ease

Amethyst
Bay
Citrine
Devil's shoestring
Hematite
Howlite
Jasmine
Molasses
Quartz, rose
Salt
Tourmaline, black

Astral Projection

Astralgus root
Cannabis
Crystal, quartz
Damiana
Dittany of Crete
Ginkgo
Huckleberry
Jasmine
Jasper
Lotus
Marjoram
Moldavite
Mugwort
Mushrooms (Psilocybin)
Opal
Poplar (Balm of Gilead)
Skullcap
Tiger's eye
Valerian
Wormwood

Banishing & Releasing

Aconite
Angelica
Asafoetida (Hing)
Belladonna
Charcoal
Clay, bentonite
Cloves
Datura
Feces
Garlic
Graveyard dirt
Hematite
Hemlock
Henbane
Hydrangea
Jet
Mugwort
Nails, iron
Nettles
Nightshade
Obsidian
Onion
Onyx
Pepper, black
Peppers
Poplar (Balm of Gilead)

Potato
Rue
Salt
Salt, black
Snakeskin
Spit (Saliva)
Sulfur (Brimstone)
Urine
Vinegar
Wasp's nest
Wormwood

Boundaries, to establish

Dragon's blood
Eggshell
Nettles
Salt
Yarrow
Tourmaline, black

Cleansing Negativity

(*See* "Negativity, to cleanse")

Confidence, to invoke

Bee pollen
Beeswax
Borage
Carnelian
Citrine
Coca
Coffee
Dragon's blood
Ephedra
Honey
Mullein
Rattlesnake
Yarrow

Creativity, to inspire

Agate
Beeswax
Jasper
Rowan

Sunflower
Sunstone
Sesame seed, white

Curses, to break

Agrimony
Ammonia
Angelica
Anise
Asafoetida (Hing)
Bamboo
Beer
Bergamot
Bitter weed
Blueberry
Burdock
Chili pepper
Cinquefoil
Datura
Devil's shoestring
Dill
Egg (Chicken)
Eggshell
Fern
Galangal
Huckleberry
Hydrangea
Hyssop
Mint
Myrrh
Nettles
Oak
Patchouli
Pennyroyal
Poke root
Rose geranium
Rosemary
Rue
Salt
Salt, black
Saltpeter
Solomon's seal root
Squill
Sulfur (Brimstone)
Thistle
Toadflax
Tobacco
Urine
Valerian
Verbena
Vetiver

Vinegar
Wahoo
Wintergreen
Wood betony
Wormwood

Death Magick

(*See* "Spirit Work")

Depression, to relieve

(*See* "Sadness, to relieve")

Disagreements, to mend

Broom
Catnip
Cinquefoil
Damiana
Dandelion
High John the Conqueror
Honey
Mercury (Quicksilver)
Myrrh
Pennyroyal
Quartz, rose
Rowan
Selenite
Sugar
Valerian

Divination

Angelica
Anise
Azurite
Bay
Broom
Calendula
Camphor
Cherry
Coffee
Copal
Damiana
Eyebright

Frankincense
Kava
Labradorite
Lapis lazuli
Moonstone
Mugwort
Obsidian
Poppy
Sage of the diviners (Salvia)
Tiger's eye
Yarrow

Dream Vision & Protection

Aloeswood (Oudh)
Amethyst
Azurite
Calendula
Cannabis
Cinquefoil
Coconut
Copal
Dittany of Crete
Frankincense
Garnet
Graveyard dirt
Hagstone
Heliotrope
Hops
Jasmine
Kratom
Labradorite
Lavender
Marigold
Mastic
Melatonin
Moonstone
Mugwort
Peppermint
Poppy
Rose
Thyme
Vervain
Yarrow

Emotions, to regulate

Anise
Abalone
Agate, moss
Jasmine

Kunzite
Lavender
Malachite
Molasses
Oak
Peach
Peridot
Sage
Serpentine

Energy, to inspire

Angelica
Bee pollen
Beeswax
Citrine
Dragon's Blood
Ginger
Honey
Lemon
Lime
Lotus
Myrrh
Orange
Sunflower
Yarrow

Fear, to ease

Basil
Carnelian
Citrine
Clover, red
Molasses
Nettles
Rhodonite
Salt
St. John's wort
Yarrow

Forgiveness

Honey
Hyssop
Molasses
Mugwort
Quartz, rose
Rhodonite
Sage
Sagebrush

Salt, sea
Sugar
Wormwood

Gossip, to stop

Adder's tongue
Alum
Baking soda
Chia seed
Cloves
Lily
Pepper, Sichuan (Szechuan)
Lobelia
Mullein
Pepper, Szechuan (Sichuan)
Slippery elm
Tobacco
Violet

Habits, to break

(*See* "Addictions, to break")

Happiness, to promote

Amethyst
Catnip
Celandine
Chrysoprase
Cyclamen
Hawthorn
High John the Conqueror
Honey
Hyacinth
Lavender
Lily of the valley
Marjoram
Meadowsweet
Morning glory
Purslane
Quince
Saffron

St. John's wort
Turquoise
Witch grass
Zircon, yellow

Hex-breaking

(*See* "Curses, to break")

Invisibility

Aconite
Agar-agar
Algae
Amaranth
Bloodstone
Cat hair, black
Chicory
Edelweiss
Fern
Hazel
Heliotrope
Kelp
Mistletoe
Poppy
Seaweed
Touch-Me-Not (Sensitive plant)
Witch hazel
Wolfsbane

LGBTQ+ Magick

(*See* "Queer Magick")

Loneliness, to relieve

Aloe
Apple
Cinquefoil
Cloves
Nettles
Quartz, rose
Roses, pink
Thorns

Luck, to reverse bad

Aventurine
Bayberry
Feverfew
Lucky hand root
Vervain
Vetiver

Necromancy

(*See* "Spirit Work")

Negativity, to cleanse

Agate
Clary sage
Dragon's blood
Feathers, black chicken
Florida water
Hyssop
Parsley
Pine
Piñon resin
Quartz, rose
Rue

Negativity, to protect from

(*See* "Protection Against Evil")

Nightmares, to stop

Anise
Chalcedony
Chrysolite
Citrine
Dreamcatchers
Hagstone
Hyacinth
Jet
Lepidolite
Mugwort
Mullein
Purslane

Rosemary
Rue
Ruby
Salt
Snakeskin
Thyme
Topaz
Vervain

Overwhelm, to calm

Agrimony
Amethyst
Cedar
Cypress
Hematite
Ice
Kyanite
Lavender
Molasses
Peridot
Quartz, rose
Rhodonite
Rose
Sage

Past Life Regression

Amethyst
Ammonite
Bay
Bloodstone
Eyebright
Fossils
Honeysuckle
Juniper
Kyanite, black
Labradorite
Lilac
Petrified wood
Rosemary
Tiger's eye

Protection Against Evil

Agate, dzi
Agrimony

Anise
Antlers
Asafoetida (Hing)
Belladonna
Bluestone (Bluing)
Bones, animal
Brick dust, red
Cactus
Camphor
Cat's claw
Claws, animal
Cloves
Cobwebs
Datura
Dragon's blood
Eggshell
Foxglove
Garlic
Hagstone
Hairballs, cat
Hamsa (Hand of Fatima)
Hawthorn
Hemlock
Henbane
Henna
Hyssop
Lemon
Nazar (Evil eye)
Mandrake
Mayapple
Mirrors
Mullein
Nails, iron
Nettles
Nightshade
Obsidian
Onion
Onyx
Owl pellets
Pepper, black
Peppers
Pitcher plants
Quills, porcupine
Rue
Sage
Salt
Salt, black
Snakeskin
Spit (Saliva)
Talons (animal)
Thorns
Tobacco

Touch-Me-Not (Sensitive plant)
Tourmaline, black
Urine
Valerian
Venus flytrap
Vinegar
Wormwood
Yerba santa

Quarrels, to mend

(*See* "Disagreements, to mend")

Queer Magick

Amethyst
Ammolite
Honey
Lavender
Opal
Persimmon
Quartz, rainbow
Shells, mollusk
Starfish
Tourmaline, rainbow

Releasing

(*See* "Banishing & Releasing")

Returning to Sender

(*See* "Reversing Energy")

Reversing Energy

Agrimony
Alder
Asafoetida (Hing)
Blackberry
Devil's shoestring
Eucalyptus
Feathers, black chicken
Hydrangea
Lemon
Lemongrass

Rue
Sage
Salt
Salt, black
Salt, Epsom
Vetiver
Wood betony

Sadness, to relieve

Amethyst
Anise
Borage
Carnelian
Catnip
Cinquefoil
Citrine
Clary sage
Cypress
Eyebright
Frankincense
Hawthorn
Honey
Lavender
Life everlasting
Maple
Myrrh
Oats
Rosemary
Sage
Salt
Sandalwood
Sand dollar
St. John's wort
Sunflower
Turquoise
Vervain
Willow, weeping
Yew

Self-love, to increase

Catnip
Flax
Ginseng
Life everlasting
Quartz, rose
Rhodochrosite
Rose
Rosemary

Sunflower
Thyme
Vervain

Sleep, to aid

Agrimony
Cannabis
Chamomile
Cinquefoil
Elder
Hops
Kratom
Lavender
Linden
Melatonin
Moonstone
Mushroom, amanita
Narcissus
Opium
Passionflower
Peppermint
Peridot
Poppy
Purslane
Rosemary
Thyme
Tourmaline, blue
Valerian
Vervain

Spirits, to protect against

Anvil dust
Asafoetida (Hing)
Benzoin (Loban)
Boneset
Camphor
Eucalyptus
Garlic
Iron
Onion
Rowan
Salt
Salt, black
Sulfur (Brimstone)
Tourmaline, black

Spirit Work

Acacia
Alder
Apple
Acacia
Amethyst
Anise
Apple
Bay
Bones
Boneset
Carnation
Coltsfoot
Copal
Cypress
Dandelion
Elder
Flax
Florida water
Frankincense
Grains
Graveyard dirt
Henbane
Holly
Jasmine
Lily
Mugwort
Mullein
Myrrh
Myrtle
Nails, coffin
Oak
Passionflower
Pomegranate
Poplar (Balm of Gilead)
Pipsissewa
Rose
Rosemary
Rosewater
Rum
Sandalwood
Sweetgrass
Teeth
Tequila
Thistle
Tobacco
Whiskey
Willow
Wormwood
Yew
Yerba santa

Trauma, to heal

Amethyst
Bloodstone
Ginkgo
Quartz, clear
Quartz, rose
Quartz, golden healer
Rosemary
Rowanberry
Valerian

Visions, to induce

Ayahuasca
Angelica
Bay
Cactus, San Pedro
Cannabis
Coltsfoot
Crocus
Damiana
Eyebright
Frankincense
Kava
Morning glory
Mugwort
Mushroom (Psilocybin)
Mushroom, amanita
Sage of the diviners (Salvia)

Bibliography

Auryn, Mat. *The Hex Appeal of Activism* (*For Puck's Sake* blog). Web: July 9, 2017. http://www.patheos.com/blogs/matauryn/2017/07/09/the-hex-appeal-of-activism.

Baab, Lynne M. *Fasting: Spiritual Freedom Beyond Our Appetites*. IVP Books, 2006.

Belanger, Michelle. *The Psychic Vampire Codex: A Manual of Magick & Energy Work*. Llewellyn, 2007.

Betz, Hans Dieter (editor). *The Greek Magical Papyri in Translation: Including the Demotic Spells*. University of Chicago Press, 1996.

Beyerl, Paul. *The Master Book of Herbalism*. Phoenix Publishing, 1984.

Buckland, Raymond. *Buckland's Complete Book of Witchcraft*. Llewellyn, 2002.

Campbell, Joseph (editor) and R. F. C. Hull (translator). *The Portable Jung*. Viking Penguin, 1971.

Cave, Nick. *Faith, Hope & Carnage*. Picador Paper/Pan Macmillan, 2023

Coughlin, John J. *Out of the Shadows: An Exploration of Dark Paganism & Magick*. Waning Moon Publications / 1stBooks Library, 2001.

Crowley, Aleister. *777 and Other Qabalistic Writings*. Weiser, 1986.

Cunningham, Catherine Lee. *Moon Musings: Lunar Poems*. Independently published, 2023.

Cunningham, Scott. *Cunningham's Encyclopedia of Crystal, Gem & Metal Magic*. Llewellyn, 1996.

Cunningham, Scott. *Cunningham's Encyclopedia of Magical Herbs*. Llewellyn, 1984.

Dass, Ram. *Remember; Be Here Now*. Hanuman Foundation, 1978.

Day, Christian. *The Witches' Book of the Dead*. Weiser, 2011.

Digitalis, Raven. *Esoteric Empathy: A Magickal & Metaphysical Guide to Emotional Sensitivity*. Llewellyn, 2016.

Digitalis, Raven. *The Everyday Empath: Achieve Energetic Balance in Your Life*. Llewellyn, 2019.

Digitalis, Raven. *Planetary Spells & Rituals: Practicing Dark & Light Magick Aligned with the Cosmic Bodies*. Llewellyn, 2010.

Digitalis, Raven. *A Witch's Shadow Magick Compendium*. Crossed Crow Books, 2022.

Digitalis, Raven, and Konstantin Bax. *The Empath's Oracle*. Llewellyn, 2022.

Farrar, Stewart, & Janet Farrar. *A Witches' Bible: The Complete Witches' Handbook*. Phoenix Publishing, 1981.

Freuler, Kate. *Of Blood & Bones: Working with Shadow Magick & the Dark Moon*. Llewellyn, 2021.

Greer, John Michael. *The New Encyclopedia of the Occult*. Llewellyn, 2003.

Grimes, John. *A Concise Dictionary of Indian Philosophy*, SUNY Press, 1999.

Herkes, Michael. *Glamstrology: Discover Your Signature Style With Astrology*. Llewellyn, 2024.

Holland, Eileen. *Holland's Grimoire of Magickal Correspondences: A Ritual Handbook*. New Page / Career Press, 2006.

Iles, Judika. *The Element Encyclopedia of 5000 Spells: The Ultimate Reference Book for the Magical Arts*. HarperElement, 2004.

Katriel, Tamar. "Lefargen: A Study in Israeli Semantics of Social Relations." In *Language and Communication in Israel: Vol IX*. Edited by Hanna Herzog and Eliezer Ben-Rafael. 31–51. Routledge, 2001. https://doi.org/10.4324/9781351291040-4.

Kraig, Donald Michael. *Modern Magick: Twelve Lessons in the High Magickal Arts*. Llewellyn, 2010.

Kynes, Sandra. *Llewellyn's Complete Book of Correspondences: A Comprehensive & Cross Referenced Resource for Pagans & Wiccans*. Llewellyn, 2014.

Ledesma, Cecilio Blanco. "Kahu." *Medium* (blog) August 8, 2023. https://medium.com/@cecilledesma_20547/kahu-ae37d36358ee.

Lochtefeld, James G. (editor). "Nazar." In *The Illustrated Encyclopedia of Hinduism, Vol. 2*. Rosen Publishing, 2002.

McLaren, Karla. *The Art of Empathy: A Complete Guide to Life's Most Essential Skill*. Sounds True, 2013.

McNevin, Estha. *Opus Aima Obscuræ*. Tradition materials & lesson notes. 2003–2019.

Melody. *Love is in the Earth: A Kaleidoscope of Crystals*. Earth-Love Publishing, 1991.

Moon, Alissandra. *Shadow Alchemy: Shadow Work & Spiritual Alchemy for Witches & Lightworkers*. Raven Moon Academy, 2024.

Prower, Tomás. *Morbid Magic: Death Spirituality & Culture From Around the World*. Llewellyn, 2019.

Roderick, Timothy. *Dark Moon Mysteries: Wisdom, Power and Magic of the Shadow World*. Llewellyn, 2016.

Silverknife, Zanoni. *Lessons in Georgian Wicca, 101-104*. Class handouts & lecture notes. Missoula, MT, 1999.

Starhawk. *The Spiral Dance: A Rebirth of the Ancient Religion of the Great Goddess*. Harper, 1989.

Tenebris, Frater. *The Philosophy of Dark Paganism: Wisdom & Magick to Cultivate the Self*. Llewellyn, 2022.

Van De Car, Nikki. *Shadow Magic: Unlocking the Whole Witch Within*. Running Press/Hachette Book Group, 2023.

Wendell, Leilah. *The Necromantic Ritual Book*. Westgate Press, 1991.

Worth, Valerie. *Crone's Book of Charms & Spells*. Llewellyn, 1998.

Yronwode, Catherine. *Hoodoo Herb & Root Magic: A Materia Magica of African-American Conjure*. Lucky Mojo Curio Co., 2002.

To Write to the Author

If you wish to contact the author or would like more information about this book, please write to the author in care of Llewellyn Worldwide Ltd. and we will forward your request. Both the author and publisher appreciate hearing from you and learning of your enjoyment of this book and how it has helped you. Llewellyn Worldwide Ltd. cannot guarantee that every letter written to the author can be answered, but all will be forwarded. Please write to:

Raven Digitalis
℅ Llewellyn Worldwide
2143 Wooddale Drive
Woodbury, MN 55125-2989

Please enclose a self-addressed stamped envelope for reply, or $1.00 to cover costs. If outside the U.S.A., enclose an international postal reply coupon.

Many of Llewellyn's authors have websites with additional information and resources. For more information, please visit our website at https://www.llewellyn.com.